THERE'S ALWAYS A DRAMA

LUCY WHITE

LUCY WHITE

Copyright © 2023 by Lucy White

All rights reserved.

No part of this book may be reproduced or used in any manner without written permission of the copyright owner except for the use of brief quotations in a book review.

www.lucywhite.xyz

Disclaimer:

This book is based on a ridiculous true story. Everyone in it is real, but I've changed their names for obvious reasons.

LUCY WHITE

Dear Ben,

Don't worry, everything will be fine.

(Hopefully)

Author's Note

Welcome, I'm Lucy and this book contains reflections of mine, and my fiancé Ev's, calamitous Euro Trip. Like madness to magnets, disaster attracts us, or rather, we attract it. Sometimes laughable, sometimes devastating, but always a story worth sharing.

Ev and I began our whirlwind of a relationship when we met at senior school. From classroom crushes to best friends to fiancés, he's always been my person. Over the last decade we've not only shared a love for travel, but also a shoulder-shrugging problem-ignoring attitude to adult life, which always results in a lot of fun for us but tends to exasperate those around us, most humorously my older brother, Ben. Our devil-may-care lack of realism repeatedly gets us into trouble, and thus my anxiety kicks in, always a little too late.

We both came from families who love to travel, and throughout our childhoods they spoke so highly of its importance, so we were bound to get wanderlust and be eager to explore.

My parents met when my mum, at nineteen, set off from a tiny English village to work a season in the south of France, where she would fall in love with my thirty-year-old dad who owned *Sunseekers,* the holiday camp she intended to work at.

Ev's parents, after just months of being together, set off on a globetrotting trip through India and then on to Australia. How better to fall in love and learn every nice (and nasty) detail about someone all at once?

The difference between their travels and ours is that whilst theirs were mostly harmonious, ours seem to have disaster after disaster. To quote my mother-in-law, *"There's always a drama."*

THE EURO TRIP

DEMONIC HALO

HANGER FURY

COMPLETELY SORTED

GEEK-CHIC BOHO-MINIMALISM

A REALLY CUTE SNIFFER DOG

ENDLESS VERTICAL COIL

SCULLING A SCHOONER

UNEXPECTED TREASURE

GYPSY GUTTER

BARE BUMMED SQUATTING

IDIOTIC DENIAL

CHICKEN CRATES

WELCOME TO RETOX

IDIOTIC SIDE OF THINGS

COMPLETELY CLUELESS

EVERYONE FIRST CLASS

ENIGMATIC ESCAPADE

The Euro Trip

"Happy Birthday!" I smiled, shuffling around to sit upright in bed.

Ev yawned dramatically. "What time is it?" he moaned as he rolled away.

"Present time!" I squealed. Normally a babbling over-sharer, I'd found it painfully hard to keep this from him, so, naturally, I couldn't wait a moment longer.

I reached over a mountain of empty pizza-boxes on the bedside table and haphazardly pulled at a protruding brown envelope. I span back around in excitement, ignoring the hollow thuds of the boxes clattering to the floor.

"Sit up." I instructed, as I passed the envelope to him.

Lazily he pulled himself up and squinted towards the curtains, "Seriously what time is it, Goose?" (Goose- a name he's called me for as long as I can remember, hopefully due to the fact it rhymes with Luc (Lucy) rather than my likeness to the hideous honking farm bird).

I ignored him and waited expectantly.

Painfully slowly he lifted the sealed edge.

"Hurry up!" I grinned, trying desperately to play it cool as I watched the love of my life open his twenty-first birthday present.

At last, he pulled a hand drawn poster from the envelope. On one side showed a colour-blocked map of Western Europe with a wiggly red line drawn across it. He looked at it quizzically, his thick eyebrows pulling together.

"Turn it over." My patience had run out.

The other side explained his present much more clearly, or at least I thought so. A decorated and overly detailed list of dates, destinations and transportations.

"I don't understand." He stared at me, still not fully awake.

"We're going on a trip!" I screamed with excitement.

I watched his eyes widen as the lightbulb in his mind buzzed on. He scanned the page again, this time taking in our upcoming adventure. I was pleased he seemed legitimately surprised as I had in fact already told him. Truth be told, I'd found the secrecy so impossibly arduous that I had faltered. I'd already told him every impeccably-overplanned minute detail, but he had been on an exceptionally high dose of morphine whilst recovering from major spine surgery, so it didn't really count. He hadn't mentioned it since, and I wasn't certain whether he'd not really understood the first time or was just pretending and would fake shock when his birthday arrived. It was too early for his acting to be this good, he'd definitely forgotten.

"When?" he beamed.

"1st of September," I pointed to the top of the page, where it clearly stated that. "Three and a half months from now, you'll be fully recovered."

Following his surgery, we'd hardly done anything out of fear of re-damaging his back, plus he'd been out of work and therefore out of money for months by this point. It had been hard for him to be so cut off from the world, and hard for me to watch him that way so this was our reward.

"That's amazing." He paused, "You know I haven't got any savings, and my work isn't back to normal yet." He was a plumber, not the best profession for a man with a slinky, now massively weakened, spine.

"Yeah, I've paid for all the accommodation and the trains, buses, coaches, boats and planes. Plus, I'll save some money, so we'll be fine!" I beamed.

For a few seconds he just looked at me, wondering how a university student had afforded all of that, and would be able to save any more but not wanting to appear ungrateful he engulfed me in his arms and squeezed so hard I thought I was going to implode.

Looking back to the itinerary, Ev said, "That's a lot of stops."

"Yeah, we move quite quickly. We're going to seven European countries; some have a couple of stops. Kind of like interrailing, but not just trains. It was easier this way." Easier? What I meant was I didn't understand the interrail ticket system so instead had planned to rush us around chaotically via various modes of transport.

"The Euro Trip." He reread the bubble written title and then grabbed his phone to check the time, "Fucking hell is four AM. I'm going back to sleep."

He lay down and pulled me into another overpowering bearhug, "Thank you so much Goose, this is just what I needed."

"I know." I whispered.

Demonic Halo

After months and months of meticulous over-the-top planning, (1. to challenge the doubters' concerns of my forward thinking, and 2. with the aim to avoid any possible disaster) we landed at Biarritz airport on a beautiful, bright afternoon. The Euro Trip had finally begun.

Not a cloud was in the sky; within seconds of stepping outside another million freckles dotted up my arms, legs and all over my pale face. My skin's never-ending game of dot-to-dot now levelled up.

Where better to begin our adventure than in this hidden jewel on the Southwestern coastline of France? Where the Pyrenees Mountains melt into the Atlantic Ocean. Where surfers swarm the never-ending beaches to ride rolling waves. Where we would camp and party on the beach and begin an easy-going traveller life. Yeah right.

Eager and fresh faced for twenty-two days of freedom, I gleamed with pride at how my plan was finally undergo, and thought to myself even if *some* things go wrong, "how much drama could there be?"

What a naïve assumption.

I was the most organised I had ever been, not a hard comparison from the woman who's lost more house keys than teeth in her life; evidently, I'd tried extremely hard to contain my scattiness for the benefit of our trip. However, it transpired that was much easier when comfily confined behind the safety of a screen at home rather than on the road living the adventure.

Ignorant to what was ahead, I proudly held a folder containing every ticket, map, and booking form we would need to manoeuvre ourselves smoothly through peaceful countryside towns, crowded cities, and coastal paradises. Now fully recovered, Ev was the muscle of the operation.

Balanced like a Buckaroo he was loaded up with every possible thing we would need, and plenty we wouldn't. If an item somehow had a link to travel or camping or hiking (like we'd ever go hiking) or anything vaguely along those lines, no matter how tedious the link, it was in the bag, (tent, stove, blow-up mattress, skateboard).

Consequently, Ev stood with my brother's hand-me-down traveller's backpack protruding comically from his, recently healed, spine. He glanced at me through his black wayfarer Rayo-Banos, smiling like a giant tortoise bathing in the sunlight. We definitely looked the part if nothing else.

Feeling like nothing could go wrong, we stepped out of the airport hand-in-hand and headed for the bus stop. I am the planner; Ev is the do-er. I'll supply the information and he'll make it happen, or not. So, in theory my part was done, and now I blindly followed him through the honking maze of airport traffic to a well-hidden bus stop.

Page one in my folder showed a bus was arriving in approximately six minutes. It would take us to the train station where we could continue our journey to the small village of Messanges, famous for its large flat beaches and monstrous waves.

However, after just two minutes, Ev was rolling a fag.

"I'm going back into the airport to get a drink, wait here. I won't be long." He can't smoke without a drink. It was a luxury that delayed us consistently throughout the trip, and, more so, in life in general.

"You don't have enough time," I panicked, "We'll miss the bus."

My timetable had not made allowances for smoke breaks, which was an unforgiven oversight as we rushed from place to place.

"No, it will be fine. Be back in a minute. Don't go anywhere."

"But-" he was already gone.

Obviously, we missed the bus. My foolproof folder-packed plan had been disrupted instantly. This should have given me an insight into how the next few weeks were going to go, and a heads up that over-planning isn't as great as it seems, but that lesson took a while to learn.

As you can imagine, I was *slightly* annoyed, so I stood several feet away from him with a sulky expression slapped across my face, as we waited for the next bus.

"It's your fault." We battled like toddlers in trouble.

The power of annoyance only your partner can wield is truly something. Anyone else could replicate their exact actions and you'd forgive them breezily, but the one you love the most and choose to spend all your available time with seems to be the one that is not so easily forgiven. Twelve minutes later, the next bus arrived and now slightly less begrudged we hopped on.

After not too much of a delay, we arrived at Biarritz train station and accessed our pre-booked tickets via a machine inside. Page two of the over-packed folder held the tickets' access code. I was doing well with my information organisation thus far.

We proceeded to wait on the platform; the sun was shining gloriously. Positivity radiated out of us as we were now well on our way to stop number one: a coastal campsite, promising beach parties and surf lessons. I'd envisaged a cheesy American beach party atmosphere, no shoes, beers on the beach, and some guy with long wavy hair playing an acoustic guitar around a flickering fire. I couldn't wait to be right in the midst of it.

I had come across this campsite online, by pure chance. I'd been searching for a cheap place to camp for Valentine's weekend trip earlier in the year (a disaster for another day) and without much effort it lured me in with its proximity to the beach, surfboards to rent and scenic bike trails, so much so that I booked this stay without a second thought, and thus the entire Euro Trip came to be.

The train was prompt and after lugging all our necessities (chairs, plates, pillows, towels that dry you so quickly they leave your skin feeling uncomfortably clammy, hairdryer) on board, we managed to get window seats. We spent the next twenty minutes admiring everything we passed and excitedly pointed things out to one another as if we had never left the house before; "beach", "fisherman", "nice house", "dog". Finally, we were away exploring and revelled in this childlike enjoyment.

Alas, when I began tracking our movements on my phone a glass-shattering awareness crumbled upon me.

"Ev, the sea is on the wrong side," I nervously announced.

He looked at me silently, waiting for an explanation or, more hopefully, a punchline.

"We're on the wrong train." I explained further.

"What do you mean?" He stared at me blankly.

"I mean we're going the wrong way. We're on the wrong train. We need to get off. We're going to be lost." I felt my anxiety taking over, my blood was rushing around my body at an accelerated speed. I stood up looking for a solution.

This wasn't the plan. I had a plan. A very well organised and structured plan. I do not like it when things don't go to plan. I looked to Ev to see if he shared my panic.

"Bollocks." He replied, eyes still admiring the sights through the window. For a man who hates to be lost, his reaction didn't match my nervous energy.

Overall, we were not doing so well; we were two for two with journeys not going to plan. I was trying not to stress but it suddenly dawned on me that I may find this trip a little testing. As an over-the-top dramatic worrier who crumbles at any minor inconvenience, I hadn't considered the problems we could face and consequently how I would react.

It was too late to re-evaluate. We were here now and evidently things were going to go wrong.

Instead, we rushed off the train, bought new tickets, and then bundled onto a different train this time heading in the right direction. We travelled back past the dog, nice house, fisherman and beach, this time minus the excited narrations.

In the near future, we had buses, coaches, trains, boats and flights to catch on much tighter schedules. I felt like maybe I had overestimated our ability to stay focused, or more likely my ability to plan a cross country adventure.

At last, we deboarded at our desired stop. I had read online that the best/ easiest way to get to the campsite was in a taxi and would cost around fifteen euros. Easy!

Leaving the station, we wandered over to the cab at the front of the awaiting ant line.

"Bon-jour. s-il-vous-plait, camper." Awkwardly I tried to converse with the driver in French but without the necessary skills to do so I quickly settled for repeatedly pointing at the campsite logo, (which, of course, was printed and slotted into my lifeline folder) and hoped for the best.

The bald driver nodded slowly; his eyes gleaming malevolently. Pretending not to notice his hungry stares, we hopped in.

We were near the sea and knew the campsite was too, so stupidly this filled us with confidence that the journey wouldn't take too long. We gazed out of the windows, admiring the town and pointing out different bars and restaurants that we could visit, buzzing with that unmatched start of adventure energy.

This trip was big for us, we'd been together just two years, and for the second half of that I had been living fifty miles away from our hometown whilst studying at university. This was much needed uninterrupted time together, in a space that was just ours, kind of. The tent was borrowed and many of the hostels I'd booked only offered shared rooms, but there was no one else here who knew us and demanded our time. Plus, it would lift Ev from his slump, and could possibly teach me to relax a little.

I'd decided this trip would set the standard for a life of travelling together, if we could prove (to ourselves and *everyone* else) that we could breeze through this then we would have no barriers for exploring further, and for longer - forever maybe?

I suppose I was right in some ways, it definitely set a standard.

The cab went on. We came to the edge of the town, *nearly there*, I thought. Campsites are usually tucked out of the way of the busyness. *The cab went on*. We saw a motorway in the not-to-far distance. *The cab went on.* We looked at one another slightly concerned. *The cab went on,* right onto the motorway. We squeezed each other's hands and uncomfortably faked smiles so the other one didn't stress, but both sets of eyes were now fixed on the ever-increasing fare metre. *The cab went on.* Fuck. Fuck. Fuck.

We were stuck within a money stealing moving vehicle with no idea of where we were, or how long we would be driving for. Both phones were now dead so there was to be no more checking of google maps. Was the driver lost? Or had I been misinformed? Maybe we'd got off at the wrong train station. All this silent speculation raced through my mind as the panic reappeared in my stomach. No lessons on relaxation just yet then.

At last we turned off the motorway. But, of course, *the cab went on.* Now, we were frantically looking at one another, at the metre price, out of the window and back to each other, desperately searching for a solution to this increasing worry.

The one, *small but important*, thing I had failed to plan for was spends. As a uni student my income was sparse, and this trip had already cost me a lot of money. I'd managed to save a bit more but definitely not enough. Ev had been back to work temporarily before we set off, but consequently had months of debts to pay back. This meant that between us we had only taken nine hundred euros, plus my brand-new shiny credit card, "just for emergencies." Nine hundred euros would go a long way in Thailand, Cambodia, India, and many other popular backpacker havens but wouldn't go so far on the pricey route I had planned, which of course included a couple of nights in the most expensive European country of them all: Switzerland.

We had learnt the hard way how easy it is to whittle away money in some other expensive European cities on previous holidays. On more than one occasion we had completely run out of money, leaving us panicked and desperate to be rescued, which bizarrely each time we were.

On our first ever trip together, to Lisbon, after just two nights we spent all of our combined money, leaving not a penny. Which meant we had no way to get to the airport to catch our flight. When all of a sudden, an American stockbroker approached us and offered to pay an extortionate thirty euros for one roll-up, sorted! Or a few months later when we massively overspent on our first night in Barcelona, and we woke up hungover and full of deep regret. But then a long-lost uncle got in touch with Ev in order to gift him a few hundred quid! It's barely believable but is one hundred percent true, and thus I was filled with enough confidence (idiocy) that we'd be okay this time too.

In an ideal world our nine hundred euros would have been evenly split across the twenty-two days, allowing us a daily budget of about forty euros.

I had imagined us living a bohemian on-the-road style life, not needing much and cooking colourful meals. I had already paid for all our transport and accommodation so really that money should have been enough for cheap food and a cultural experience or two. But this isn't an ideal world and as much as I wished it, we weren't free-spirited low-maintenance travellers.

So, there we were, two skint twenty-one-year-old "backpackers" trapped in the back of a very expensive cab in the middle of what felt like nowhere. Wonderful.

The cab went on and on and on. Eventually, we joined a wide, seemingly endless road lined with fir trees that towered above us on either side. The soaring trees and monotonous straight-on driving made the road feel infinite. Time was ticking on yet nothing felt like it was changing. Somehow, we had entered some weird psychedelic time-warp that was costing us our precious euros by the second. On and on and on and on.

After years of driving on the tree-trimmed-treadmill the cab pulled off the road and into the campsite. That beachside explanation that had sold me all those months ago had been a rather large exaggeration. For the second time that day I was questioning my route planning.

Now we'd stopped, the driver turned to us and gave a wide devilish grin, the metre price hanging above his head like a demonic halo. A bright, luminous two-hundred-euro halo. Two hundred! Our *budget*-backpacking trip was off to a great start. Resentfully, we parted with the cash, which evidently shot a large hole in our funds. Feeling hollowed we got out and Ev loaded up again.

Quietly we walked to the check in desk, neither one of us wanting to mention the crumbling plan or decaying budget.

A middle-aged woman with thick curly hair and a ten-foot-wide smile welcomed us kindly. She showed us to our pitch enthusiastically , talking the entire time about everything and anything that crossed her mind. "You're from England, how lovely. I've been to England, yes I had baked beans! We went to a show too. You must love the rain - haha!"

We just listened, her word infiltration stunning us silent.

As we walked further, I noticed a significant lack of tents, not one. We were in a motorhome city. Of which its occupants were all aged sixty-plus. Not quite the beach party atmosphere I had hoped for then.

It wouldn't have been so bad if we didn't have the most ridiculous tent in the entire world: Illuminous blue and so small that we could only half inflate our double mattress, if we didn't want it to bust through the tent's flimsy walls. It was less mattress and more, *saggy bag of air.*

"Okay this is your pitch, nice one with lots of trees. Put the tent where you like, toilets and showers are just over there-" she pointed to a building about ten metres away, "Have fun!" and without waiting for our response she bounced back to the front office, still nattering endlessly as she went.

After all of two minutes assembling our temporary home, we were ready to eat. We had, of course, been dragging a stove around in our Bag Of Wonders all day, and had planned on cooking to save money but decided after the day we'd had we should *treat ourselves*. A motto we find very hard not to live by, even when we definitely do not need to be treating ourselves. Good day? *Treat ourselves.* Bad day? *Treat ourselves.* Almost out of money with no idea how'll we buy food and rent for the month? *Treat ourselves.* Miserable about being skint? *Treat ourselves.*

We were already down a huge amount of the budget, so why change now? We have a way of being that fun-loving money-spending devil on each other's shoulders at just the right, or wrong, time.

"I don't want to cook; shall we go out for food. It's been a long day." Ev looked at me with an expression of I-know-it's-wrong-but-lets-do-it-anyway, a face I knew all too well.

"Definitely." I didn't mention that I'd forgotten gas for the cooker so therefore cooking was not yet an option anyway.

So, with the plan to dine out luring our hungry stomachs away, we ambled back to reception and asked a gangly teenage staff member for any recommendations.

In response he sheepishly laughed, "There's a holiday park down the road. Nowhere else."

The spotty-faced boy shot a sideways smirk to another teenager lounging next to him with his feet up on the counter. I assumed they were the sons of the Mother-Hen who had greeted us, they had inherited her thick curls but not her enthusiasm.

We began trudging our way back down the eerie road to arrive at the French equivalent to a chav filled Butlins. Promptly, we ordered the least deadly looking thing on the menu and settled down to watch the in-house entertainment of fighting children and despondent parents. In desperate hope for some holiday fun, we began sinking some thick coral coloured syrup that was lazily impersonating wine.

Though disgusting, it did the job as a few drinks, and a ropey meal, later we were cheerful again.

"I can't believe we're finally here." I smiled at Ev.

"Here?" he laughed looking at our dismal setting.

"Well, no not here, but on the trip. I've been thinking about it for so long. Today went a bit wrong but we'll just make sure we look things up and double check before we go to the next places. I've booked all the other journeys anyway; it was just getting from the train station I hadn't planned." Rose (coral wine) tinted spectacles blurring my vision.

He puffed his cigarette and sipped the disgusting wine, "Sure." He chuckled, shaking his head. Clearly he had better foresight than me.

We walked arm in arm with a bag of take-away booze back to our laughable desolate campsite. Day one was over, and already we had spent way too much money, realised my planning was slightly off, and consequently had no idea what to do for the next few days. But we were full of wine and had smiles slapped on our tipsy faces, foolishly believing that things were bound to get easier.

Hanger Fury

Our second day came quickly and uncomfortably. The three of us (Ev, me, and the huge backpack) were squashed together like sardines in a nylon tin.

"Morning," I rolled towards Ev which in turn rolled him towards me as the air in the mattress displaced.

"Morning. I'm so hot." He panted.

It was uncomfortably hot. Our skin stuck together as each outward breath raised the tent's core temperature.

"Get up," I pleaded for him to move away from me.

"You." He pushed me towards the tent's half-zipped door.

Instead, I pulled the air-stopper from the mattress and laid back down lifeless until I felt the hard floor and sharp rocks stabbing violently into my back.

From then it became a routine we followed each sizzling morning in the tent. The unrelenting pain made us more inclined to get up, plus the release of air provided a few more precious inches for us to move around.

After being awake for all of three minutes, it occurred to us that we had no food and were very, *very*, hungry. The joyous aromas wafting from our towering neighbours' breakfasts didn't help. So, we pulled on some clothes, abandoned everything we owned, and walked to reception to enquire about renting the precariously positioned bikes outside of their hut. Instead of being greeted by the smirky teenagers of the previous evening the larger-than-life Mother-Hen was back and she smiled graciously.

Her presence comforted me, she had that feeling of unconditional care. She'd fix your problems or make you a snack or tuck you in as if you were one of her brood.

"Bon-jour," I grimaced with awkwardness, "We'd like to rent those bikes out the front."

"Oh wonderful! That's just great. How about ten euros each for the rest of your stay?" At least someone was considering our budget.

Instantly we set off. Cycling miles down the long, empty road we had arrived on the previous evening, only this time we could truly absorb the bleak scenery rather than our eyes being transfixed to the taxi metre. We kept going and going, pedals to the metal, or more the unsurfaced rocky road. My bike heaved as I forced the pedals round and round, clacking and screaming as they went. The flat tires puffed out every ounce of energy they could muster. It quickly became evident why the camp-mother had been so pleased. Clearly, no one had ridden these bikes for years. Maybe she thought we would take them to their screaming graves and therefore get them out of the way. But no, we pushed on.

Eventually we found a bit more life, cars mainly, and I had never hoped so much to find a shop- Ev doesn't do so well when hungry; it's as if the growls in his stomach fuel his desperation. A simple problem, and usually one that's easy to solve yet he reacts with such fear each and every time his belly needs refilling. His pedalling was getting quicker in his (now beyond desperate) search for food, I knew if I didn't fight to keep up, I'd inevitably get lost and never see him again.

Thankfully, after about twenty minutes of forceful cycling we found a supermarket. Outside there was a hotdog truck withholding a cleanliness rating of less than zero, from what I could judge, but of course that didn't deter Ev.

"I'm getting a hotdog; I can't wait any longer. Want one?"

Twenty euros for an unsanitary hot dog? Sure, why not? We were haemorrhaging money anyway.

"Really?" I tried not to look too disgusted but clearly failed.

"Suit yourself." He wandered over and ordered an identified meat tube in a bun and covered it in ketchup.

He devoured it in seconds, but I was well aware that this wasn't enough. Time was of the essence.

We entered the shop, and I quickly loaded Ev's welcoming arms with breakfast supplies; bread, sausages, gas for the cooker (how lucky that they sold that!) everything we needed.

Foolishly, I took a detour to leisurely peruse notebooks, it seemed a necessary purchase and I *needed* just the right one. The fractions of Ev's eyes that I could see through his cradled pile of groceries filled with rage, he bellowed (his voice is extremely sonorous naturally) "Just choose one!" I did so and unashamedly rushed to the till.

Ev's hangry mood took a while to subside, combined with his stubborn nature caused him to insist on carrying all the shopping on our ride home.

The way people become sassily independent to show passive aggression is bizarre and totally counterproductive, but he was not the first to do that, and certainly won't be the last. The, *I don't need your help,* attitude resulted in him having to ride the entire way one-handed, with the other laden down with supplies- I could practically see his veins bursting out of his extended forearm.

I didn't argue. I am wobbly on bike, to say the least, and didn't really think I could cope with cycling whilst holding something, and the ramshackle handlebars definitely couldn't support anything further. On reflection, I think he secretly knew this, but wasn't up for admitting kindness at this point.

We arrived back and I immediately set about preparing breakfast in our dusty pitch. Not muddy, nor grassy, just excessively dusty. The kind of fine dust that floats in the air and noiselessly arises in puffs as you step on it. Consequently a light brown dusting now covered everything we owned.

Quickly I attached the gas canister to the cooker and set about assembling a breakfast feast. As they cooked, the sausages smelt mediocre (at best) but any food would have done by this point. My stomach gurgled and a frown had taken permanent residency across Ev's already sun kissed brow.

Finally, the food was ready, and it was time to eat.

"Want me to do it?" I offered as I watched Ev chasing the slimy sausages around the pan with a pair of watermelon pink tongs.

He ignored my offer and at last caught one. Carefully he lifted it out of the pan and onto the paper plate folded in his thick hand. He repeated this with the next five sausages until they all rested within his grips. That is until all six decided to kamikaze into the dust below. The only way to describe what remained would be to imagine dropping a wet, sticky lollipop into the inside of a vacuum that had just finished servicing a Saharan campsite. You cannot undo, or fix, the mess that you are left with. Nothing could be saved after it entered the dust.

He erupted, booming out "FOR FUCK'S SAKE!" in an otherwise quiet campsite. Normally a very peaceful -loud- but peaceful man, was now in a full-on hanger fury. He threw the tongs forcefully across the floor, thus covering them too in dust, "This is so ridiculous! Why are we even here?" He boomed.

I looked up at his unneeded eruption and unnecessarily added fuel to his fire, "You're ridiculous." A childish retaliation to a dramatic reaction.

With that he stomped off to sulk around the campsite. I began to think this trip had not been such a good idea. I sat wondering if we would make it out together, or even alive, as I added two slices of bread to the greasy sausage pan.

After a short while he returned. It was hard to take his anger seriously as he slumped onto his one-foot-tall, three-legged camping chair. Mum and I had so much fun buying ridiculous camping gear in the weeks leading up to the trip - these *Poundland* chairs being a prized possession. (Other ridiculous purchases consisted of a toaster attachment for the stove (that we never could decipher) and rain macs that before use doubled up as keyrings - but after use had absolutely no intention of being that small again, therefore making them more of a burden than a benefit.)

In hope of reconciliation, I shuffled my chair uncomfortably close to Ev's, "I love you," I smiled adoringly.

I was trying to ease his mood I guess, but evidently, it came across as more gloating-bitch than lovesick-puppy (he later told me that is the one of the most irritating things I have ever done). He was trying to revel in his anger, and I was not allowing it. Eventually, he forced a smile in return, and we chewed through extremely oily bread together, trying to hide our gags as the oil slid down our throats and mixed with the syrupy wine still resting in our bellies from the previous night. Clearly, we weren't the natural adventurers we had hoped to be.

"What shall we do today?" I tried to lighten the mood.

"You mean we're not scheduled to be anywhere." Ev teased.

"Well, I thought we'd be near the beach, so we'd go there but we're not. So, I'm not really sure what to do. I don't want to sit here all day."

"We could get to the beach." He oozed confidence with this statement.

"Really?"

"Yeah, I reckon. On the bikes." he winked at me, knowing my incompetence.

Greasy bread ingested, and now feeling more than slightly sick, we grabbed our passports, remaining cash, and all other important things, shoved them underneath the deflated bed, half-zipped up the tent (so it didn't get too hot), and got back on the rickety bikes. I inwardly feared that they would fall into a thousand pieces' mid-journey.

Obviously, the campsite wasn't as close to the beach as we had thought, but we desperately hoped it was still reachable. Back down the monotonous road we went. We cycled past the morning's shop and on further until, finally; we saw signs! Actual road signs! And then, a main road. I had never before been so pleased to see a beaten-up BMW with a leery man leaning out of it.

As we cycled further, my stomach turned with the swirly syrupy wine and greasy bread concoction. I pleaded with myself not to be sick, violent vomiting mid cycle wasn't really the image of the care-free traveller I was so desperate to be.

Soon we came across a fruit vendor, brightly coloured fruits of all shapes and sizes residing in mismatched wooden crates. It was the perfect postcard picture. We stopped to browse.

"I've bought us some peaches to eat at the beach." Ev smiled as he hopped back onto his bike. I hadn't bothered to demount as each time I did I managed to painfully scrape the back of my calf on the exposed metal pedal.

A strange beach snack I thought, almost asking for a repeat of the morning's sausage incident but thought better than to question it. The pause gave my stomach time to settle, and I rejoiced in the fact that I would not chunder in front of my loved one, for today at least.

A lot more painful pedalling later we hit a dense forest, with a winding stony track through the middle, *don't fall off*, I thought to myself repeatedly as we progressed inside.

We cycled up and down countless hills through the forest, screaming and cheering like howler monkeys warning off intruders. Quickly the bikes built momentum, racing down and flying us up the next mound over and over again. My recently settled stomach flipped as if I were tearing through the skies on a rollercoaster. Surrounded by coniferous trees and shadowed by the thick foliage, I almost forgot about the endeavour to find the beach. Up and down the hills rolled, with us tearing over them. That giddy excitement from the previous day was weaving its way back in.

After what could have been days, the trees thinned, and we now faced a steep hill sprinkled with sand. Eagerly, we pushed ourselves up. My heart was racing, not solely because of the hundreds and thousands of miles we had cycled; at last we saw what we had been hoping for. An endless golden beach and huge crashing waves, with an added bonus in that it was filled with people our age, and not a motorhome in sight!

The sea air hit me like a thunderclap in the middle of the night and melted the tired ache right out of my legs. Feeling so relieved to have found that bit of perfection that had drawn me there in the first place.

"Yes!! Ev you found the beach!" I squealed with delight, "This is the one, from the pictures. I can't believe you found it." I wrapped my arms around his middle.

Carelessly, we dropped the bikes and darted for the sea, stripping as we went, then finally diving into the icy shallows. The waves were unbelievably huge; we hadn't noticed the danger-red no swimming signs flying from the lifeguard's tower, and before I knew it, I was tumbling over and over and over inhaling copious amounts of seawater.

In true hero style, Ev pulled me out and dragged me to a safer part of the beach. I quickly shattered any hints of glamour as I lay beached and spluttering with my bikini tangled and twisted in unflattering angles, now exposing everything it was designed to hide. My tangled curls slapped across my face like an enamoured sea monster whilst I fought to regain control of my breath. Just the look I was going for as I lay on the beach with the love of my life.

He, of course, took it all in his stride and his golden skin glowed in the midday sun. Ev smiled at me adoringly as I caught my breath and slid away the reems of seaweed stuck to my limbs in a failing attempt to appear somewhat cool-beach-chick rather than full on goof. By this point he was well aware that I was an ungraceful calamitous, but I was still desperate to seem debonair, or mysterious or anything other than a hot-mess. Unfortunately, this was far from likely.

"I've noticed something." He said looking down at the maladroit he'd just pulled from the sea.

I panted and looked up expectantly.

"You just do things without thinking, if you just give things five minutes or even just a minute's thought, you'd do it so much better. You're all speed, no haste. And then you'll spend a year overthinking every mistake afterwards. I mean look at your leg! Why are you just dragging it across the pedal and continually cutting yourself, slow down."

I looked up wide eyed and wordless, like a baby who had just been explained the rules of quantum physics.

He laughed and slumped down into the sand next to me to roll a fag.

I ignored his attempts at life advice and instead set about asking him a barrage of "What ifs," and "Would you rathers,"

(What if a tsunami happened right now what would you do?)

(What if that man over there ran over and tried to abduct me?)

(Would you rather never speak again, or say all of your sentences backwards?)

(Would you rather have legs as long as fingers, or fingers as long as legs?)

He played along with as much excitement as an overtired dad on a post-Christmas car journey, whilst we drank beers in the sun admiring our, now, ideal setting.

"Now I'm so happy we're here. And actually here!" I looked around beaming.

"Me too. This is going to be amazing, Goose. Thank you."

A wide toothy grin spread across my face, as I felt quietly proud that things were starting to fall into place. Maybe we'd be alright after all.

We rolled about in the calmer current until the blazing sun lazily hid behind a billow of wispy clouds. The feeling of joy was overwhelming. This is what we live for, lulling together in the sea, watching the world drift by as the sun waves above us.

Slowly the sun began its descent, so we retired to the sand to eat our much-needed peaches. Consequently, it was the best peach I have ever tasted, and since then it has always been our beach-snack of choice, just don't let it touch the sand.

Feeling more at peace, we cycled leisurely back to the campsite, stopping on the way to buy beers and ingredients for dinner. We laughed the evening away and I even managed to cook successfully on the tiny stove without sacrificing anything more to the dust.

Regularly, we swapped seats as, coincidentally, the tiny chairs were bike-seat shaped and not at all comfortable after a day of cycling on ten-thousand-year-old bikes. The more comfortable, luxurious option was a tea-towel atop the dust with a thin, knobbly birch tree as a backrest; we both rejoiced in the relief it gave our aching bodies. Two days in and we were behaving as if we'd been on the road for years, evidently, we had a lot to learn. All the while we were playing endless rounds of a Norwegian card game my housemates had taught us, keeping a running total of wins- that now years later we continue to add to. I wish I could say I was winning.

I smiled to myself as we went to bed that night, thinking if this was a snapshot of what the next few weeks had to offer, then it was going to be glorious. Everyone had said how ridiculous it was to carry all this stuff through seven countries. And how impractical to camp after hours on trains, boats, and planes. But I knew then, even if they were possibly-slightly-right-in-some-ways, that we were right to go and that our adventures began here in this dusty deserted campsite.

COMPLETELY SORTED

Waking up the next morning in Camp Dust, we decided we'd better spend the day making a new exit plan (rather than another risky taxi-ride as planned) as the following afternoon we were to catch a cross-country-coach to Toulouse from Bordeaux Station (which was considerably far from where we were). Seeing as my arrival plan had been less than ideal, we thought it best to ask locally.

For most of the morning, we cycled around, taking a different route this time, until we came across a tiny, picturesque village. Temporarily we were distracted by ice-cream, so sat and enjoyed it in the sun, lazily watching the world go by. I felt ten years old again, cycling around with no aim or purpose, just taking it in turns to lead the way. Frequently whilst travelling, I find myself feeling like a child. Being free from ordinary routine and order transports me right back to a time when life was simpler, an immense desire of many adults, but often it's masked with a fear of losing control. The freeness that existence can be often appears just out of reach, as when the mundane is obliterated there comes an uncertainty and lack of structure that only seems socially, and often personally, acceptable whilst exploring. A strange thought, to be free only when far from home and often lost, skint, burnt or jet lagged.

Remembering we actually did have something we needed to do, we resumed our search and eventually found a bus stop. I'd worked out that if we could get a bus to St Vincent De Tyrosse station, then we should be able catch a train to Bordeaux, and there we'd board the coach to Toulouse. It departed at four-pm, so ideally we'd arrive slightly before then and it would cost less than we paid on arrival. Ideally, being the operative word.

Astonishingly, the bus we needed left from this stop and went directly to the train station, perfect! Or not quite. The following day was a Sunday- buses don't run on Sundays in tiny French villages- or at least not in this one.

It was my turn to strop now. In true toddler style, I threw myself across a stone bench to sulk, utterly deflated.

"What are we going to do?" I moaned. "We're going to be stuck here. We can't get another taxi or we'll run out of money. And we need to be at Bordeaux station before four tomorrow, or that's it! Plan ruined! And then what? We'll just live here forever." My dramatic inner narrative jabbered.

If we missed the coach to Toulouse, we would be off schedule, a schedule that I had thought was faultlessly planned, but clearly not so much. It would mean missing prepaid buses, coaches, campsites and all the rest. Again, another reason not to over plan, it can cause more stress trying to meet deadlines and therefore make the desired relaxation of holidaying much harder to achieve.

"Well, we could live here forever, or, we could go and ask in there." Ev rolled his eyes at my dramatics as he pointed towards a travel agent's just a stone's throw from where we stood.

I regained my "cool" "Yes, we could do that." I jumped up and began walking over, with him chuckling behind me.

"Bonjour!" A woman with slick black hair and dark purple lipstick greeted us.

"Bon-jour," I blushed. "I was hoping you could help us." I proceeded to explain our current predicament and plans for the following day.

"Okay. And where are you staying?" she fluttered her dark eyelashes, looking straight through me and over towards, a none-the-wiser, Ev.

I felt my sunburnt cheeks get hotter.

"We're camping," I added quietly.

"Camping! Where?" her strong accent added to her judgement.

I pulled my folder from my backpack, flicked over the first few pages to show her the campsite's logo. To which she then had to search on her computer. I assumed they didn't get many campers asking for help.

Once she finally understood where we were staying, she guaranteed us a way out the following day. Her plan began with a taxi collecting us in the morning and taking us to a neighbouring town to catch the bus to the station. Seemingly sorted, we thanked her and left, not thinking of it again.

Continuing our afternoon of cycling we stumbled across a market, in which we strolled for a while and bought more unnecessary crap to lug around, including a hideously bright lime-green selfie stick which neither one of us ever managed to decode – resulting in thousands of holiday snaps in which we are staring quizzically at the camera.

Finally, we headed for another wonderful evening at the beach, the waves just as cosmic as before. That night ended much the same as the previous; routine seat swapping and frantic card playing in our ridiculous O.A.P campsite as we tried hard not to sacrifice our dinner to the dust. As night three rolled in we zipped ourselves into the sweat box, three days gone and thirty percent of the budget spent. I thoughtfully reasoned that although we'd overspent thus far, "We'd stop tomorrow," and the remaining euros would last the duration. At this point I didn't even trust my own "plans" but the forethought helped me to sleep more peacefully.

******

Once again the morning came unwelcomed. However, after dragging ourselves out of our tiny home we were surprised to meet another young couple walking the campsite.

We chatted pleasantly for a bit before telling them our plan for the day. Kindly, they offered us a lift to the train station, but as we were *completely sorted*, we happily declined. Looking back, that was the stupidest thing we had done so far.

In a different manner to the initial packing, we shoved the tent, mattress, stove, chairs, plates, gas canister and kitchen sink messily into the backpack and hastily returned the bikes to reception. Mother-Hen seemed disappointed to receive them back but thanked us anyway. An air-conditioned, and temporarily, not dust covered car, was waiting for us, so we jumped straight in. I desperately hoped for a swifter journey than our previous cab ride.

Thankfully we drove for just a short while until stopping at, well, nothing. A closed sports centre, from what I could decipher. The driver asked us with a quizzical expression if this was the right place and questioned if we were sure we wanted to get out. This should have been a significant warning sign, but determined to follow the travel agent's plan, we exited the vehicle. Clearly, this was not a bus stop. We wandered up and down the road, still no bus stop.

Panic hit. A little too late, as our driver had already left. Not a soul was in sight. We were in a disconcertingly quiet village with no idea of how to progress on our journey. The roads around us were wide and empty. No buses, cars, bikes or people were anywhere to be seen. I surveyed our surroundings, something wasn't right.

I'd at least remembered to charge my phone this time, but the internet was hazy. Looking at the partially loaded map, it seemed we were not where we had expected to be. However, it seemed that we could walk to the train station. Not ideal but achievable. Eager to exit this creepily quiet place, we followed directions infrequently as the internet fumbled for connection. We walked, paused, watched impatiently as the loading circled whirred round, walked back on ourselves, then paused some more. As the internet disconnected and reconnected repeatedly, we twisted and turned unsuccessfully through sleepy residential roads. Back and forth like crazed windscreen-wipers in a blizzard. Time was ticking on and still we hadn't seen another person. Every shop shut. All curtains closed. Dead silence. It was utterly unnerving.

Alas, it was all in vain; a temporary internet high allowed us to learn that we were much further away than we originally had thought, so consequently could not walk to the station.

We were completely lost, Ev's only other hate. Hunger and being lost. So far, we had managed to experience both on his birthday trip. The trip I had planned to lift him back up after his post-op slump, a trip designed to add cheer, not stress. Yet unfortunately they would reappear frequently.

This was one of the worst times, however, as there was just so much nothing; noiseless, soulless, and empty. A blacked-out derelict vampire mansion with loosely boarded windows wouldn't have been out of place here.

Time was precious, and yet it felt like it was slipping away at an accelerated rate. Every corner we turned held more spooky emptiness and drained another ten minutes, then twenty, until we were certain this empty void would swallow up the rest of our lives.

Then, in the far distance, a man! We approached him in a hurry, desperate for a solution and wishing him to solve all of our problems, hoping for a magic genie wasn't too much, right?

"Hello! Hi! Can you help us?" I waved and flapped like an embarrassing mother waving off her child on a school trip.

"Hey." He grinned as I ran towards him, Ev pacing behind me.

"Hi, bon-jour, we're trying to find S-t Vin-cent D-e Ty-ro-sse train station." I poorly over-pronounced each unfamiliar word, "Do you know how to get there?"

Ev caught up, "Hello mate."

"Hey." The guy repeated.

"Did you hear what I said? We're lost, we've got to get to Bordeaux by four and we don't know where we are." The words were freefalling from my babbling mouth.

He stared at me. Pausing my panic, I took a second to take in who I was talking to. A caramel skinned, heavily tattooed, scruffy haired man in an oversized acid washed vest, board shorts and worn-out flip flops. Over one shoulder hung a cramped backpack covered in rips and holes. I concluded this man was not a local.

"I don't know where that station is," he exhaled deeply as if my asking had caused him great stress. "I am from Mexico. I am hitchhiking."

I frowned. Many, many questions rattled in my brain, but we didn't have time for answers.

"How's that going for you?" Ev asked, shooting me an amused side glance.

"Today, not so good, but I'm not in a hurry." He shrugged with so much nonchalance I was certain he was mocking me.

"Okay well we really need to get going." I tried to walk away.

"Wanna get stoned?" The out-of-place Mexican hitchhiker suggested.

"Have you got any weed?" Ev raised his eyebrows with intrigue.

"No, have you?"

I rolled my eyes.

Ev laughed, "No. I assumed as you were suggesting-" his sentence tailed off as he realised his explanation was pointless.

"Good luck with your hitchhiking." I smiled as pleasantly as I could muster.

The most-definitely-not-a-magic-genie saluted us silently, turned on his heels and then set off, whistling to himself as he persisted with his pursuit of inebriation by heading further into the depths of Slumber-Town.

Continuing with our quest for life, we found a pub. Spilling out of it was a cackle of elderly men who seemed to find the sight of us very amusing. Their animal sneers and menacing glares only added to my increasing worry. These weren't the type of elderly men you would smile sweetly at and wish them a nice day. These were the kind that had been hardened by a life in the pub and consequently despised the young. Deep set snarling wrinkles and fag-coated hyena howls loomed over the entrance like spiked brambles for us to fight through. Neither of us wanted to approach, but we were faced with no other option. The laughs got louder, I felt so uncomfortable that I fixed my shoulders tensely under my ears and a pained grimace took over my face. Not much *fake it til you make it* going on here.

"Bon-jour, w-w-we need to find," my hands shook with social anxiety as I fumbled for my folder.

"We're trying to find a train station; we need to get to Bordeaux." Ev finished my sentence for me.

"Can you help us; we haven't got much time." I added.

The bartender swished her blonde glossy hair over her shoulder and replied, "I don't know where we are either," using an over-the-top whiny voice to convey her faked stupidity.

Of course, this caused all the men to cackle some more. It was unnecessary cruelty from local losers, that I am yet to forgive. We waited for her to laugh it off and help us, but she just pursed her overly red lips and raised her eyebrows, before lighting a cigarette and leaning back down on the bar pretending we weren't there.

Throughout this confusing interaction, the men were staring at me with predatorial glares, and in that moment I felt completely unequipped to fend them off. Our stress, hunger, and lack of proper sleep left us unable to navigate this weird social situation, so not knowing what else to do we rushed back out of the pub through the thickets of gremlins.

Humiliated and clueless, we slumped on the curb in deflated dismay. After not too long a young couple walked past and their overtly surprised faces invited us to chat with them for a while. It seemed they didn't often have tourists in this town; they were surprised to see us. We explained how we'd unintentionally stopped there, our lack of intention seemed to be a lot more understandable. The male part of the couple kindly offered to ask mum to take us to the station, and they quickly rushed into the black of flats behind us. Minutes later he called down from their window: the mum said no. Our hopes were temporarily lifted, then dropped carelessly from their third-floor balcony to shatter beside us.

Without another choice, we re-entered the pub, this time shoulders fully inflated with fake confidence, and asked the teasing bartender to call us a taxi. I felt all eyes burning tauntingly and creepily into my exposed skin. Following a brief phone call the bartender sniggered, "My friend will pick you up. Wait outside."

Obediently we did as we were told, and sure enough my anxieties began to battle. Was she really cruel or just trying to joke and we weren't in funny moods? It was hard to know whether to trust her, and now her friend, or to try to find some other way out of this wretched place. Quietly I unloaded my worries onto Ev, who responded with, "Most people are good people," and, "I'm sure we'll be fine." Not quite the counselling session I sought, but it sufficed.

It felt like a lifetime of waiting, the relentless laughs getting louder and more malevolent as time went on. All the while our coach to Toulouse felt like it was becoming more and more unreachable.

At last the friend arrived. She was uncomfortable-to-the-eyes-thin, had long scraggly bleached hair and big sunglasses covering most of her gaunt face. Wrinkles hung on for dear life as the skin on her skeletal body drooped from her bones, hanging out of her mouth was a thick brown joint and she sucked on it shamelessly whilst surveying us. I looked around for our Mexican friend as we had accidentally found just the person he'd been looking for, but he was nowhere to be seen.

Loud music blared out of her decrepit car; the seats were bedazzled in wooden beads. She clearly was not a taxi. We got in anyway. The music stopped abruptly and after nodding her understanding of where we wanted to go, she said nothing. At all. The silence was so uncomfortably thick I thought it might suffocate us.

She seemed to drive further and further out of town, not the brief trip we had longed for. We passed vast empty fields and dreary murderous woods and then continued straight past the sign of where we wanted to go. I had made distressing peace with myself that we were going to die soon, looking at Ev it appeared he had done so too. I have never seen so many abandoned caravans as I did on that journey, I was certain we were going to be held in one until she killed us. Flashbacks of a multitude of cannibalistic horror films danced devilishly in my mind as I now wished we had spent the millions of lazy hours of our life dedicated to another, less thought intrusive, movie genre.

As we worried, she persisted to drive sporadically with no apparent care for our, or her own, safety. She weaved, scraped, honked and sped through winding country roads. The wheels clipped the curbs, wing-mirrors chipped branches as she swerved chaotically, all the while we had no idea of her intended destination. I debated sending a goodbye text to my mum but thankfully thought better of it and saved her the heartache.

After a stress-inducing forty minutes, we arrived at a train station! Not the one we wanted, however.

Almost inaudibly (she either suffered from dysarthria or was so stoned her mouth couldn't be bothered to move) she explained it would be easier for us to proceed from here. A kind reroute from a terrifying stranger. Of course, our gracious driver charged us a small fortune so, the two taxis and train tickets totalled another two hundred euros, great! Fifty percent of our budget had now dwindled but at least we were alive and somewhat on our way to stop number two.

After gorging on sandwiches from the station's café and rejoicing in our narrow escape from death, we checked for departing trains and we were in luck, just a five minute wait! At least this leg of today's journey was seamless.

Before we knew it, we'd arrived at Bordeaux and begun scouring the nearby bus stops for our coach. Desperately hoping for a smoother journey, we looked thoroughly for a bus stop resembling either the company's logo on our tickets, or with any mention of Toulouse. We found neither. Plus no one inside nor outside the train station had any idea either.

C'est super!

Geek-Chic Boho-Minimalism

It was now two minutes past four, two minutes after we were supposed to be aboard a coach to Toulouse, but instead we were slumped on the steps outside an unfamiliar train station, ready to give up all hope. Again. Who said we're melodramatic?

Five minutes passed. Then ten. Still, we sat slumped, unable to think of anything better to do.

"We've missed it Ev, we can't just sit here all day. We need to somehow get to Toulouse."

"We can't have missed it. We've been here the whole time." He paused, "Are you sure this is the right place?"

I scowled, hurt he would question my foolproof plan, then slyly checked the tickets again.

"Yes, this is the right place." I gloated.

Public buses came and went from the sparsely arranged stops, but no coach. Fifteen minutes passed. Ev went back into the station and asked again, but still no one knew what we were talking about. I read and reread our printed tickets, we were at the right station, on the right day but the coach was nowhere to be seen. Our entire day's plan and dramas that had led us there were all in pursuit of this coach and now that it wasn't here, we didn't know what to do. We weren't lost or rushing, just confused and waiting for something we weren't sure was coming. It was panic without pressure, an unusual mix.

We'd somehow managed to do our bit so now it was time (or at least fifteen minutes ago was time) for the coach to do its part of the journey.

We sat clueless for another five minutes. Then in the distance I saw it. A large black coach uncomfortably weaving through the traffic. Green digitised letters circulated across the front of it, as it edged closer I managed to make them out: TOULOUSE CITY CENTRE. We jumped to attention and fixed our eyes upon it eagerly, desperate not to lose sight as it crawled towards us.

Almost magically, as if it knew our despair, the coach pulled up and stopped directly at our feet. With its arrival, other clueless people swarmed from all over and rushed aboard.

It was comforting to see other lost travellers. Rightly or wrongly, it reassured me that we were not the problem, at least not this time. We nestled ourselves in the back corner ready for a four-hour drive and were relieved, not to mention a little shocked, that we had actually made it.

The journey was almost without any hiccups, we wrote quizzes for each other and played homemade crosswords whilst watching the world drift by, pleased that, temporarily, we were not navigating it. Sitting inside a vehicle we had no control over was a welcomed break to cycling, being lost, syphoning money and sweating within a tiny tent. Neither of us mentioned the fund situation, which was good as it definitely would have killed the recently lifted mood.

Once we were off the coach, and it was far too late, Ev realised he had forgotten a shoe. Somehow his only real pair of shoes (not flip-flops) had tumbled out of his bag mid-journey and now one lay forgotten. What made this worse was that he had already gone back on board to retrieve his forgotten tobacco but had failed to notice his lonely "Van" beneath the seat. Maybe I'm not the only "all speed no haste" person in this relationship after all.

The next day, we held a funeral-style farewell for the remaining Van as we deemed it would have been ridiculous to carry the surviving one with us, not like the necessary ski socks, mini fans, full set of saucepans and portable shower.

It was getting dark, but we decided to eat before heading to the next campsite. Yet as we were on the outskirts of the city, not right in the heart as we had expected the coach to stop, finding somewhere to eat was easier said than done. Aimlessly we wandered up and down poorly lit avenues in desperate hope for something to soothe our hunger, and some wine to take the edge off. In only the way a hungry mind can, we daydreamed aloud of food as we became more and more lost.

"I want cheese on cheese on cheese, and pizza." I longed.

"I want that too and a steak. And pasta. And chicken." Why we felt like starved orphans after just a few hours without food I do not know, but it didn't bode well for our desired traveller life.

Eventually, we found a zapping-neon-lit café so after ordering a bottle of wine and a disappointingly-carbless-meal, we sat outside to people-watch, inventing dramatic backstories for strangers as they passed us.

It was my turn: "That's Michelangelo, he's thirty-four, lives alone and works as a chef. He's trained for years but he's not very good, poor guy. He was going to propose to his boyfriend, but he left him for his gym instructor. So tonight, Michelangelo is seeking revenge."

"This is taking a dark turn," Ev chuckled.

"It's the hunger, it's changing me." I exhaled dramatically.

Thankfully Michelangelo's story was interrupted by the arrival of our much-needed wine, then surprisingly real drama unfolded before us.

Two haggerty men stumbled around the street before us desperately trying to pickpocket unsuspecting passers-by, which was unsettling to say the least. Thankfully, they were not particularly good.

The aspiring thieves had a routine that didn't change, no matter how many times it failed. The older of the two would select a target, nod towards the younger who would try to cause a blockage in the path thus reducing the target's speed. The older would then creep from his shadowy lair and look for something of value that he could reach in a timely fashion.

Not once did we see him snatch anything, each time he just peered into people's bags from a comical distance, much further than his arm's reach.

Evidently, he didn't have the confidence needed to pull off the heist. Their Fagan-style coats and leery smiles seemed to warn potential victims too. I wouldn't have been surprised if they'd begun chanting a catchy show tune about their reasons for potential theft, thus inviting a hidden camera crew to appear and document the over-acted performance.

After an unsatisfying meal of cold cured meats and an over vinegared leafy salad, not the hot carb overload we had craved, and *a lot* of wine, we realised that once again time had passed us quickly. This was not ideal as we had been instructed to arrive at the campsite before eleven. Already at twenty to eleven, we raced in a mad panic to the closest taxi rank and joined an extensive queue.

As we waited impatiently, I continually checked the time, each minute passing quicker than the next. I'd come to learn on this trip that

Time is a cruel player, moving faster the later we'd become and slowing down in situations I wished would end, teasing us menacingly with its omnipotent power.

Each check of the Time, on my more-cracked-than-whole phone screen, assured me that we would in fact arrive much later than eleven. I wondered what this would mean for us. I so hoped we would still be let in and given a pitch to camp in, we really couldn't afford to find somewhere new. Plus, I didn't fancy scouring the now dark city for a place to sleep after consuming not enough food and more than enough wine.

At last, it was our turn but of course, we were refused! Over and over and over, due to our abundance of stuff. This was seeming to be a repeated concern from other people, frustrating as we (Ev) were the ones (one) who had to carry it. The reason why this was a problem was lost in translation, but the rejection was crystal clear. So back in line we went, again and again.

When at last we were accepted, this driver found another grievance: the destination. How reassuring. He offered no verbal explanation of his hesitation, just seriously raised his eyebrows, and forcefully rubbed his sweaty forehead. His lack of enlightenment only led to my overactive mind creating farfetched scenarios of the horrors that awaited us. Desolate and isolated? (again) Ungracious hosts? Rabid animals? Drug den? Murder maze?

After much reluctance, on his part, and many sentences started and then regretfully stopped, causing yet more fearful suspense, we finally set off out of the city and into the night. As we watched the streetlights diminish and the deep black of the night take over, we got closer and closer to campsite number two.

After a silent fifteen-minute drive we came to a gravely stop. I peered through the window surprised to see towering iron gates, secured together with a thick chain and a comically large padlock. If anything screamed "Do Not Enter" it was this. Our driver buzzed perpetually on the intercom until, at long last, a voice crackled through.

The voice and the driver joined in an un-matrimonial heated discussion whilst we waited awkwardly in the backseats. Obviously, they were arguing in French, so we were none-the-wiser to the problem at hand. It appeared our driver had forgotten we were even there as he grew more and more irate with the crackly voice. Suddenly he spun around and gestured for us to get out; he waved his hairy hand with disgust as if we were flies buzzing around his lunch.

Obediently, we stepped out and he left in a hurry, without even a hint of a glance back. Watching him drive away, I wondered if we had been abandoned by all of humanity and left to fend for ourselves outside this sombre gated world.

Thankfully, I didn't have to wonder for long as three hench twenty-something men meandered towards us and unlocked the gates. Once the huge padlock had been removed, they greeted us with venomous grins and creepily beckoned us to enter. I could barely see past them, so my brain was still desperately panicking about what lurked beyond. On reflection, I don't know why we were so compliant, the entire setting screamed midnight massacre.

A few more steps into the darkness took us to a dimly lit office and who I presumed to be the lingering potential murderers' dad sat inside. We all entered and stood uncomfortably close together, I felt like they were presenting us as prey to their master.

Now with the help of the dusky office light I felt certain all of these men were related, the resemblance was undeniable. Four matching hook noses and a full set of blackened irises set low beneath quickly retreating hairlines. They shared the menacing look of comic book criminals.

Aggressively, the dad (the familiar crackly voice) demanded our passports and didn't respond well to our initial resistance, mainly due to our uncertainty of their current location.

Eventually, we did as we were told and rooted them from the bottom of the big bag, much to the humour of the three lads. They sneered and cackled at us continually as we tried to talk. Not the most welcoming way to treat new guests but their vicious-guard-dog act obviously boosted their own egos, clearly that was more important. Their over-the-top hostility suggested their bark was worse than their bite, but I was wary nonetheless.

I handed over our passports and he flicked through them as if pursuing a catalogue for a new sofa, twisting and turning for a better look. Looking back at us with dissecting eyes. What a performance.

"You can camp down there," the gut-busted dad panted as he lazily motioned down a poorly lit gravel track. His hand barely extended, and his fathead hardly looked up. He clearly had no intention of showing us to our pitch. He tossed the passports back, instantly turning back to the game of solitaire on his computer screen.

This unwelcoming lazy oaf couldn't have been more opposite than Mother-Hen from campsite one. The same job, the same country, yet one was all hugs and smiles and the other was spikes and snarls.

Barely informed, we walked quietly into the darkness pondering if we were going to be followed and/or killed.

After a while, and yet again passing many-a-motorhome, we reached a tiny grassy patch with two picnic benches and a tent already on one end. We decided this must be, "down there," so in no time at all, we assembled our tiny home. Our day's journey was finally complete.

Relieved to have actually made it, we sat ourselves on the bench outside our tent. Instantly we got our music playing, illuminated our head-torches, and pulled some beers from our very own Mary-Poppins-style never-ending bag, pleased to be sitting on something other than our triangular toddler-size seats.

On the other bench, about thirty metres away, were the inhabitants of our neighbouring tent. A group of girls, who looked around our age. From what we could hear they weren't speaking English, but we thought we would try to befriend them anyway, us with no real language knowledge were arrogantly aware that it was likely they could speak our native tongue.

Following a beer-fuelled discussion about the interactions between men and women, and the often-differing perceptions of them to those intended, we decided it would likely be more *kindly* received if I went over, even though I am the more socially awkward of the two. So I did.

"Hi, we're camping over there-" I hesitated mid-sentence as I felt their fiery judgement burning my skin. This was a scene right out of Mean Girls, I'd unknowingly approached a group of queen-bee-popular-nasty-bitches. Instantly they'd smelt my weakness.

"Um," I continued. "I'm Lucy that's Ev-" I pointed, and he raised a hand brandishing a lit cigarette between his index and middle finger.

Any nice normal person would have said something by now, but they all just continued staring at me, my gaze moved across each face desperate to find a hint of kindness. Instead, I was met with narrowed piercing gazes, eyebrows raised but curved cruelly back down into irritated frowns, and lips pulled downward whilst being pressed together so tightly the abundance of filler looked ready to burst its way back out. My very existence was being scrutinised as I stood before them helplessly.

"We were wondering if you wanted to join us for a drink, or-or a game of cards?" I finally finished my sentence just before my throat closed up completely.

The lead bitch, sat up so her back was perfectly vertical, crossed her arms across her chest and simply said, "no thankssssss," dragging her "s" in a suitably snakelike manner.

The other girls giggled, flicking their chins into the air just to confirm their superiority in this hideous social situation. The only other people around, apart from the Doberman brothers, and they already disliked us.

The laughable set up, head torch, and excitable friendliness obviously wasn't the geek-chic boho-minimalism I had imagined, instead it was more dorky-little-sibling-vibes.

Unsure how to react to this obvious condescension and unneeded coldness I turned away and tried not to run as I retreated to Ev. Critically digesting the rejection, I slumped down in a pit of embarrassment.

"That's their problem not yours." Ev's breezy response to my social panic was totally right but, in that moment, I felt so critically judged that his unwavering self-confidence was far from contagious. So far that I jealously resented him for it, and for making me talk to them. At this point I never wanted to talk to anyone else ever again.

"But I-"

"No but anything. You were nice and they weren't, fuck them. It doesn't matter. It's your turn." He nodded his head towards the cards on the table. I found his casualness baffling, why couldn't I be like that?

Thankfully the girls soon got into their tent and I eased up a bit. Until then every echo of laughter or awkward meetings of eyes had kept me on edge.

We played a few more games of cards and then we too clambered into our tent to sleep. It was dark, but not quiet. At all. Our newest abode bordered an enormous field and the crickets within it created a cacophonous din, which was immensely amplified as we nestled our heads into the floor. Unable to settle into a much-needed sleep, we lay awake worrying if the Dobermans had plotted anything malicious for the night ahead. Neither of us felt particularly safe, so we hugged tightly, wide eyed and fearful.

A Really Cute Sniffer Dog

The next morning we awoke from a broken sleep with screaming bellies. Rapidly we pulled on some clothes and made for the campsite shop. I'm not sure whether to call it bravery or stupidity, but Ev purchased some sort of grey meat pastry and instantly gobbled it down. Upon the sight of it, I decided I could wait until we got into the city to eat.

His willingness to eat absolutely *anything* amazes me, it's so far from my fussy food inspecting habits that I often watch him in wonder. Most of the time he's escaped harm free, but there's been a few occasions where just a couple more seconds of thought would have saved severe belly ache, and worse, for days on end. In truth, this mostly occurs after he eats something I've cooked. Fussy-eater skill-less cook is quite a combination I've thrown together and unfortunately for him, Ev seems to be my primary victim.

To our surprise, the campsite offered a free shuttle right to the heart of Toulouse. We asked the less than enthusiastic cashier what time it departed; she snarled in response, informing us that we didn't have long. Evidently working here required you to be terrifyingly callous. Whilst waiting for the bus, we befriended -temporarily- a retired Scottish couple. A mismatched pair, a short stout woman with cropped grey hair nestled under an oversized sun hat, and a towering muscular moustached man wearing a gym vest and luminous short shorts. They looked more like a comedy duo than a married couple.

Clouded by her thick accent, the sun-cream smothered wife asked us what we did for work, I replied first, "training to be a teacher," to which she cooed over and expressed that she had also been a teacher. She moved her gaze to Ev, eagerly awaiting his answer.

"I'm a plumber," he smiled.

In insulted-response, she bellowed: "THAT'S DISGUSTING!" Her brow sunk so forcefully in the middle I wondered if she could still see. Following her caricature frown, she very childishly crossed her arms and turned her back.

Flabbergasted, I struggled to contain my laughter. I could feel my face burning and my shoulders were uncontrollably pulsating. The blatant shock all over Ev's face didn't help and I burst into a fit of hysterics. What an unnecessarily unpleasant interaction. We hadn't met many people on this trip, so far, but the ones we had had made me question all I thought I understood about basic conversation and normality.

Consequently, the couple actively avoided us on the minibus, shooting just one more appalled squint as we squeezed past. Let's hope they never need a new boiler fitted; I don't think they could live with the shame.

A short bus ride from the campsite was the stunning city of Toulouse. Once we deboarded we began leisurely strolling around in the sunshine, with no aim or purpose rushing us on. After a while, we stopped for coffee and browsed through our newly purchased city map. Keen to navigate, Ev appointed me the role of sight selector. I would choose something interesting, and he would walk us there. We spent hours working our way around from sight to sight, and pub to pub. He revelled in each success and had the most wonderful day, as did I following helplessly without the slightest sense of direction anywhere in my body. I am *geographically challenged*, as my aunty Karen has correctly labelled most of the women in our family. Hence Ev's recurring instruction for me not to leave his side or move from where he's put me if he needs to go somewhere.

Once we had exhausted points of interest, and my legs, we stopped for dinner, finally we got the hot carb overload we'd been craving, and *some* wine before lazily making our way back to the campsite.

Arms linked and steps wobbly we laughed all the way to the bus station, as I barraged Ev with more throughout provoking questions:

"Would you rather be made of cheese or chocolate?"

"If I turned into a worm would you still love me?"

"What would you do if an army of bats swooped down and took me away?"

Luckily (for Ev's tired brain) we arrived just before the last bus departed, a quick flail of the arms prevented us from being left behind and the doors reopened just for us. This really was luck as neither of us had looked up when the buses were running and had both forgotten the name of the campsite (my information packed folder was safely tucked away under the deflated mattress) so getting a taxi would have been near impossible.

Hopping off the bus, we walked beside the road we had driven in the dark the previous night. Over a glistening stream, through a blooming meadow, and up to the looming iron gates- now not quite as terrifying but definitely not a warming welcome home.

******

Another morning rolled in and this time we had a long day ahead; pack up camp, get to the airport, fly to Barcelona, explore for a bit, back to the airport, fly to Genoa, find campsite three, and reassemble the site.

So it was less than ideal that I had set the alarm for seven-PM instead of seven-AM, causing us to wake up late, instantly submerged into that hideous frantic time-panic caused by unintentionally oversleeping.

"Shit! Wake up! Wake up!" I flapped.

"What? What's happening?" Ev awoke with a shock.

"Hurry! Quick, get up! I set the alarm wrong. We're late, we need to go. Now!"

He rubbed his eyes and leant forward to pull the stopper from the mattress.

As he did so an email popped up on my phone. "Oh, wait. False alarm." The panic in the tent blew away as the air escaped beneath us.

There was another minor malfunction; the airline had emailed to notify us that our flights had been changed to later in the day. Firstly, this meant we were no longer late, but it did mean we now wouldn't land in Genoa until after midnight.

"I think we should book a hotel for tonight." Ev suggested blearily as he lay uncomfortably on the empty airbag. "We're not going to be able to find a campsite in the middle of the night. Let's book a hotel then carry on the plan tomorrow."

"Good idea," I grinned. The idea of being out of this tent for over twenty-four hours sounded perfect.

After a lot of internet dramas, our rural location and crappy phone service didn't make for ideal hotel hunting, we finally managed to book a room. It cost *slightly more* than what we could really afford but it was a necessity. Day six and seventy percent of the budget was now gone, how was it possible that we had actually increased our daily spending? Thirty percent remained, for sixteen days. Two hundred and seventy euros to see us through, Italy, Switzerland(!), Germany, Austria, Hungary, Croatia and then back to Italy. All of our meals, booze and inevitable mistakes, on approximately sixteen euros and fifty cents per day. I choose not to fixate on that, and instead let the sudden promise of an actual bed lift me off our sunken air-sack and began packing with a newfound energy. Loaded up once more, we made our way to the public bus stop, we were too early for the campsite's chauffeur.

A short while later, we were in the air en-route to Barcelona. I had worked out that if we deboarded quickly, we could spend a good amount of time exploring the city before having to return to the airport for flight number two. Once off the plane, we rushed for the train. I had memorised the stop we needed to get off at; I had it completely covered. Whilst on said train, I relayed what I had found on the internet to Ev, who for some reason didn't accept it. He felt he knew the train stations in Barcelona better than the internet.

"That doesn't sound right. I reckon we get off at the one before and explore there. I think I recognise the name." It had only been a year or so since we had visited Barcelona, but we had spent most of that weekend in a booze-infused nocturnal routine, so I highly doubted his ability to recognise anything. I went along with it anyway.

Obviously, he was mistaken, and we were lost. Again. We ended up having to get on a bus to complete the journey to my intended destination, wasting an overall time of one hour of our flying visit. Now, without enough time to really do anything, we rambled Las Ramblas for a quick reminisce and then headed straight back to the airport. I found the whole situation funny (I suppose because for once I couldn't be blamed), however Ev didn't. He thinks with his stomach and the delay cost us our desired tapas lunch feast, leaving us with just incomparable snacks from a supermarket. Stomach sad, Ev sad.

Hours later, we arrived in Genoa and thankfully our bag had too. We said goodbye to it in Toulouse and desperately hoped it would join us again, but we were not wholly convinced. The budget airline, with its last-minute changes, hadn't filled us with confidence in their competence. Completely exhausted, we made our way towards the exit, longing for the comfort of a real bed. It was just steps away- I could already see the glowing lights of the hotel, attracting us like moths to a flame.

Ev, however, saw a dog. A really cute dog. A really cute sniffer dog. He wandered over and began playing with it. At once the dog mounted our big bag, which Ev was lazily dragging along behind him, causing the armed guard with the dog to shout with a military sternness,

"What's in the bag?!"

Slightly stunned, he replied that he just wanted to stroke the dog. The man's anger did not subside. He blew sharply on the whistle around his neck and two more armed guards swarmed to us. Now with unnecessary back up, he forcefully informed us that, "dog smells hash in your bag."

"What? No. We've got lots of food and a cooker and-" I tried to explain away the problem.

"He smells hash." He glowered.

"There's no hash in there," Ev raised his eyebrows dismissively, almost rolling his eyes at their superfluous anger. His casualness only infuriated the guards more. The main guard, Guard One, forcefully took hold of Ev's arm, yanking it up as if he were a naughty school child being marched to the headteacher.

With this the other two sprang into action, one grabbing his other arm and the last one snatching up our bag.

"What are you doing? There's nothing in there! Let go of him!" I pleaded.

"Hash!" The guards spat at us in unison.

"Mate, there's nothing in the bag." Ev was almost laughing at them. His reluctance to take any situation seriously is the most infuriating thing when you're on the opposing side of it. I knew that more than anyone.

I shot him the well-known look between couples of, shut-the-fuck-up-you-absolute-idiot.

He responded with the look of, but I'm right?

It was useless. Of course, he was right, I knew that. But these very angry Italian guards with guns, didn't and the more he antagonised them the longer this situation would go on.

They continued marching him along, whilst I followed frantically.

"Please, there's nothing in there. If you just look or listen to me- we're camping and have got a lot of stuff. Some food, maybe the dog smelt that? Or maybe the gas cooker?" Words were spilling out of me a hundred a minute.

Guard Three, the one with the bag, noticed our luggage tags and spoke to the others sharply.

Guard One looked at him, then to us, and asked, "Where have you come from?"

"Barcelona." Ev answered with an air of annoyance.

"Well, actually we were in Toulouse this morning, but we stopped in Barcelona briefly this afternoon on our way. We're from England originally." The speed in which my words were travelling made them totally incomprehensible, I continued anyway.

"You get hash in Barcelona." Guard Two told us.

"No we didn't!" I was now running behind them to keep up.

"You leave hash in Barcelona." Guard One announced.

Ev stifled a chuckle. I could have killed him. They very much could kill him.

"No hash!" I implored.

They marched him into a small room and locked the door behind them. Guard Three reappeared to keep watch. I stared at him in disbelief, he stared right back.

I began to babble some more; nonsensical words fell out of my mouth as I pleaded for them to return the person they had stolen. I pled his innocence, stupidity and regrets. I threatened, stamped and huffed. Then apologised and pleaded some more. No matter what I said, he gave no reaction. He kept the stern composure of a well-trained beefeater, barely acknowledging my presence, let alone my panic.

I watched the clock rigidly, each minute feeling longer than the last, Time was playing with me again. My head was full of horror, as more and more situations rushed through my mind. They were robbing him, beating him up, arresting him, smuggling him away never to be returned. Five minutes passed. Surely, my endless nagging was going to wear thin on the doorman soon. If it gets to nine minutes I'll scream, I thought to myself, pleased to have a somewhat plan in this way-out-of-my-control situation.

Thankfully, it didn't get to nine minutes. After seven painfully long minutes, a wide-eyed bewildered Ev exited the room, the only explanation he offered was, "I didn't know it was a sniffer dog."

It was my turn to roll my eyes.

He informed me that they had furiously quizzed him about our connecting flight and were adamant we brought hash from Barcelona, or left hash in Barcelona, and insisted the dog doesn't smell food "Only hash!", but after a thorough search of the bag and a lot of shouting, they realised he was harmless and set him free. The guards watched him suspiciously as he relayed this information. My usually tanned man had turned a ghostly shade of white and his booming voice had dropped ten-decibels. I shot the guards a judgemental glare and then protectively grabbed Ev's arm and scurried us out of the airport before anything else could occur.

Weirdly, we checked into the hotel alongside a mid-league (apparently) Barcelonian football team and consequently held high hopes for the room. We were not disappointed; the bed was outstanding. However, any bed would have been after camping on a half-inflated wobbly mattress for what felt like years.

I lay in bed thinking how happy I was not to be in that polystyrene prison, not to have bugs next to my head, and not to have to apologetically wake up Ev to escort me through a dark and scary campsite when I needed a wee in the night. My bladder seemed to fixate on the latter. I woke up in the early hours of the morning desperate for a wee but totally confused as to where I was, so found myself running around chaotically, crashing into each and every obstacle, whilst (unsuccessfully) attempting not to wake up Ev.

Wonderful.

Endless Vertical Coil

After lazing about in this relative luxury for a little too long, we had to rush frantically to board the coach for a quick ride into the heart of Genoa. As we sat down, I handed Ev a belated anniversary postcard, with just the words "how ridiculous" written on the back; every one of the anniversary cards I have ever given him, now nine, says the same. Because it does feel ridiculous, to be navigating the world with this person I admired unbelievably when we were at school. The well-liked loud-voiced class clown, who has become my best friend and life partner. Our world together is so fun, and filled with constant laughter and love, but yet is absolutely *ridiculous*.

At some point during the journey, I began feeling really unwell. My back teeth were throbbing, and my sinuses felt like they were about to burst. I was being viciously attacked by my own face. In aid of soothing the pain, I held my face in an unattractive jaw protruding position for the duration of the journey whilst I begged Ev to massage the ache away. Evidently, I was in urgent need of assistance, so we planned to visit a pharmacy ASAP. Thankfully, we were not too far from our destination. To take my mind off the pulsating poison, Ev chatted idly about what we could do for the rest of the day, our first full day in Italy. We settled on eating first, then swimming in the sea throughout the evening.

Temporarily distracted from the pain by a beautiful port city, we happily jumped off the coach and strolled the cobbled streets. We found a quaint, quiet restaurant and piled in with all of our baggage, ungraciously knocking into every table we passed. Thankfully, we were seated on the second floor at the very back, so only bashed into about thirteen unsuspecting groups of diners. Cringing with public humiliation and crass clumsiness, I began perusing the menu.

The beach's calmness spread lazily up to the old stone building breezing through the rectangular wind-eye beside us. Although we were completely surrounded by busy tables of patrons, it didn't have that crowded irritable feeling that inner-city restaurants often emit. Yet another reason beach destinations will always trump cities to us, we aren't striving to win the rat-race, or wanting to be involved with eleven-*erifers*, we want a simple life and that comes from slowness, and sand in your toes.

Deciding we once again deserved a treat, (one more day off budget wouldn't hurt, right?) we gorged ourselves on six courses of Italian delights, jubilating in pasta, pizza, breads, and cheeses, until we could hardly move. Peace washed over us as we drank glass after glass of Italian wine, overlooking the crystal-clear sea. The setting was idyllic, and a welcome calmness set in. Time stood still as we watched the waves move gently from our personal viewpoint, temporarily it was on my side again. The building had a castle-likeness that brought a magical feeling that I wanted to indulge in. Hands interlocked and smiles beaming, we were already in love with our temporary location.

Completely content, we decided we'd best try to find our campsite. Surprisingly, this wasn't a hard task. Just a few steps from the restaurant, we spotted the campsite's logo on a road sign. How suspiciously easy.

However, next to the logo was an almost vertical arrow pointing towards a dauntingly steep hill. That's more like it. Spiralling around the mammoth mountain was a shockingly narrow uneven road, no path and no barriers. One wrong step and we'd be over the edge and into the busy road below. Ev looked at me and back to the road, I could almost hear his thoughts discussing my lack of ability.

Wanting to avoid injury we asked a nearby taxi driver to drive us to the top. Without so much as a glance in our direction, the sweat covered man lazily replied, "Walk." So, without another hesitation, we began scaling the behemoth.

Initially, the fuzziness of the wine and the glorious sun evoked positive mindsets. But within a minute, or maybe two, my jaw and sinuses were throbbing intensely again, and I remembered our mislaid plan to find a pharmacy. What made it worse was that something that can only be described as a thick cheesy sauce began oozing out of my nose. Ev, already carrying the big bag, (containing mugs, mallets and mosquito nets) as well as his own backpack with his other holiday goods, now also took mine from me as I sobbed helplessly whilst my face attacked me from the inside. The hot sun didn't feel so good now, as tears, cheese sauce and sweat raced their way down my face.

Before long, our untrained legs were burning, neither one of us particularly fit, Ev following his recent operation and me from sheer laziness, so this was a real challenge. The wine's usual ability to make even the most boring things fun was being pushed to its limit as I tried to smile through the pain.

This was travelling, exploring and adventuring all the things I'd wanted, right? It was a lot harder than I'd thought it would be. I much preferred the beers on the beach part to the actual moving around element, especially this time. Again and again, it occurred to me that I wasn't the adventurer I'd thought I was.

As the hill got steeper I thought it likely that we would die before ever seeing the top. Each step added to the last, but my body seemed to stay put, I was on a well disguised treadmill with no promise of ever getting off.

The cheese sauce now flowed freely from both nostrils, my face hurt like hell, and the clammy evening sun only added to the extreme torture. I was a different person than the one who had begun this climb, there was no positivity, or much fluid by that matter, left within me. This time I did send my mum the final goodbye, in text form, however I forgot to press send until later in the day when it was accompanied with a more positive update, to which she found wildly amusing.

Ten minutes up, we were exhausted and dizzy from the endless vertical coil.

"I give up! I can't go any further." I threw my arms in the air. "I'm staying here."

Ev turned to see me slumped on the floor with nothing blocking me from tumbling off the edge.

"Get up, you can't stay there." His eyes were full of pity, but I knew his patience was temporary.

I looked back at him: exhausted, sweating and covered in backpacks.

"I can't do it." I whimpered.

"You have to. There'll be beer at the top."

I knew he didn't know that to be true, but trusted his confidence and kept going for another five minutes until our saving grace, in the form of a middle-aged man in an old creaky car, pulled up next to us, "You want lift?" The stranger offered and without any qualms, we piled into his car. At this point, even kidnap would have been better than any more climbing.

He reassured us that we were nearly at the top and we got the feeling we were not the first people he had rescued. He drove us the remaining four hundred yards and, like a true hero, accepted nothing but a thanks and turned back down the mountain. We wondered if he just spirals up and down all day, saving idiotic tourists. We stood sweating and dishevelled for a moment, my face still pumping like Stromboli.

Barely recovered and dripping with sweat, we headed to the "welcome" hut, where, once again, we were greeted less than affectionately.

"You were meant to arrive last night!" an angry face glared up at us. The man it belonged to was barely five-foot, his eyes only just visible through the hut's window. I explained about the flight and that I had emailed to let them know our amended booking details. That wasn't good enough, judging by how bitterly he talked at us as he logged our arrival on his ridiculously outdated computer. I hadn't seen a screen that thick in more than ten years, it was a miracle it still worked.

Begrudgingly, he informed us of the shuttle bus to and from the beach, which now sat conveniently at the bottom of our mountain as unfortunately we had missed the last bus down. However, the last bus up wasn't for two and a half hours. If we could get ourselves back down, we could spend some time at the beach and then return back to the top with little physical effort. I wasn't certain my wobbling legs would carry me back down, but we were keen to spend some time at the beach. It was worth the risk. Now in a rush, we sped off to pick a pitch,. We settled on a central one that gave a magnificent view of the mountains surrounding us. Experts now, our site was assembled in no time and lazily we pushed our things inside.

Thankfully, our descent back to the beach was much calmer than our struggle up. Partly due to gravity's powerful pull making us travel at great speed, and partly due to a well-hidden less-steep path that stupidly was only sign-posted at the top. A resident refusing taxi-driver, perilous trek, unfriendly host and secret escape route really came together to suggest this campsite did not want visitors.

At last, we were frolicking in the sea and the stress, pain and sweat washed away. The cool refreshing waves soothed my now swollen, and a burnt shade of vermillion, face. My looks and feelings weren't matching up; I felt all the joys of travelling return in one euphoric hit yet looked like an oozing beefsteak tomato on pasty legs. Ev of course matched the surroundings. As I admired the stunning beach; layers of smooth grey pebbles covered by sparkling aquamarine water he glided through the water, his golden skin glimmering and dashing smile mirroring the water's sparkles. For not the first time I wondered how we'd been matched, but in fear of bringing an unwanted realisation I kept quiet. We (the calamity and the Adonis) splashed about, admiring our surroundings. The beach was small, about fifty metres wide and not too populated, the perfect place to end our roller-coaster of a day. After lolling about for a while, we retired to the sunbeds to drink cold beers in the setting sun. Calm once again set over us, and beer blurred the pain in my puffy face. Glamorous not so much, but I was at total peace.

Suddenly remembering the return bus, we jumped up and darted around the corner to the meeting point, only to be greeted by the stony face whom we had encountered on arrival. This time we had a full view of his miserable face, and low-down body, as he frowned up at us. Had he followed us down? Or had someone returned to collect him, and he failed to give us the same option? Either way, he wasn't pleased to see us, especially as we had only just made it in time.

Sheepishly, we shuffled onto the bus. As we climbed higher and higher, I gazed out of the window, this time enjoying the views the ascent offered and feeling a lot more serene. We spent yet another evening playing cards, and without another option dined on three-euro pizzas in the campsite café, (that was definitely a budget friendly meal) whilst befriending other campers as we chatted about our travels. Yet again most were motorhome owners and at least double our age, enjoying retirement by driving from country to country. What a dream! We tried not to sound too incompetent as they shared stories from their trips so far. Instead, we kept our comments brief and mainly just discussed locations, they didn't need to know we'd spent almost all of our money, been lost, scared and stupid. No, I'd save those character damning stories for a book years later.

Although our stay in Genoa was such a whirlwind, it holds a special place in our memories as the serenity, beauty, and tradition came together so perfectly that we felt like we had entered another world. The contrast of beach bliss to city carnage was amplified drastically as we moved so quickly between the two throughout this trip, but this beach was the peace in the midst of the storm that we had so needed.

Sculling a Schooner

Reluctantly, we woke up early with another eventful day ahead. However, the realisation that this was our last campsite made getting up so much easier. When planning the trip, I had started with good money-saving intentions, trains, buses, and campsites but as it went on, I had opted for more ease and comfort thus booking more hostels and flights, at this moment I was very thankful for the squander. I had considered following one of the millions of pre-made tried-and-tested routes I'd seen online, but didn't like the "confinement", no, instead I thought it would be better to follow a vigorous self-made, hard to navigate and evidently flawed itinerary.

Deciding we no longer needed the mattress, we planned to offer it to the grumpy man from the previous day. A communal campsite mattress? Who wouldn't want to borrow that during their stay? However, when we went to visit, he wasn't there to accept it. Kindly we left it outside his hut as a surprise departing gift. An unwanted thanks for his unneeded hostility.

Considerably lighter, we headed to the station to catch a train to Milan. A pitstop for a quick explore and an Italian lunch, on our way to Lauterbrunnen, a municipality in the Swiss Alps.

We admired the sights from our leisurely journey,

"We should travel Italy one day." Ev suggested.

My stomach bubbled with excitement, I was unsure whether this trip had put him off ever travelling with me again, "Yeah? We could start at the top and work our way south."

"Just stick to the coast I reckon, beach to beach drinking wine and eating pizza."

"That sounds perfect." I stared at him adoringly, finally the fog of his last few months had completely lifted.

"Maybe we'll get a motorhome and celebrate our retirement cruising the coast. Everyone else seems to have one," he teased, "Plus less chance of things going wrong." Following our many opportunities to observe them, we'd noted that it seemed a significantly less chaotic way to travel. But then that may have been less to do with mode of transport, and more to do with the realism that comes with the typical age of the inhabitant. Or the money.

Milan consisted only of a very cheesy-pasta lunch that cost the earth. We had little time to explore as we were hustled so much outside of the station, and easily convinced into buying useless crap, (a wooden fruit bowl that collapses perfectly flat, more Rayo-Banos because can you ever have too many? And a genuine "silver" bangle, or two…) that once replenished, we had to head straight back to catch the next train.

We were leaving Italy having spent eighty-five percent of our entire travel fund, and now heading into Europe's most expensive country with just over one hundred euros, not forgetting the remaining fourteen days that followed. Fantastic. A quick Google of, "How to make money fast," left me no richer and with a headache after listening to one too many whiny-voiced con artists try to entice me into their pyramid schemes. I may or may not have been sucked into a matched betting subscription and consequently lost more of our precious euros.

On top of this looming worry, my sinus pain was back with vengeance. No matter how much beer I tried to dull it with, it would not subside. Resulting in a large portion of this journey being narrated by my pitiful sobs. By this point, the cheese sauce was gushing like an infected waterfall from my nostrils, and as much as Ev pretended not to notice, he later told me it was the most disgusting thing he had ever seen/ smelt in his life. This from the man who had spent months living in close proximity with other men in the sweating heat of outback Australia, with no money for soap or washing powder, and no driving desire to keep themselves or their shared bedroom (in which they weed in the sink) clean, was a harsh revelation.

But he was right, it was truly revolting. Why must my own body attack me this way? I was trying so hard to be carefree and have no worries, but I was in fact full of worries once more.

This was a long journey with a lot of train changes, so we were excited to see the final one. Especially because it looked like a handcrafted toy straight out of the seventies, making us feel like giants whilst travelling inside it. Perfectly painted tiny carts with swirly patterns gently bumped us along deeper into the Swiss countryside. As we got closer to our destination, the stunning landscape came into view, dove white mountains soared into the sky and a glistening, rapid lake ran beside us. It was more beautiful than we could have imagined and we wondered why we had never heard of "Lauterbrunnen" before; we were there by pure chance (I liked that the hostel had interior wooden beams, and wooden flower boxes on the windowsills, therefore planned it into the route). Not a classical travel guide reason to visit somewhere, but in this case it worked out surprisingly well.

Once off the toy trains, we jumped on a bus that took us further into the fairy-tale. It was breath-taking. The landscape was framed by climbing mountains that were dotted with perfectly positioned houses so flawless that they looked like models, a trickling roadside waterfall splashed beside us. I was half expecting woodland creatures to carry my bag and dress me in a sparkling ball gown.

Without assistance from any friendly furred flunkeys, we made our way to the hostel, immensely pleased not to have to set up camp. In complete awe of our location, we sat outside to drink some beers and take it all in. Unable to locate a pharmacy, the alcohol had no choice; it was going to have to work as my medicine for one more day. As beer was still refusing to help, I resorted to vodka to save the day. I poured it in and hoped for the best. Swollen face aside, we felt at utter peace in this unexpected scenic treasure.

However, two truckloads of eighteen-thirties soon obstructed our picturesque view. Within seconds of them stepping off the coaches, we could hear that they were Aussies and instantly knew we were in for a good night.

"Alright Guys?" Bill, a larger-than-life trucker dressed in the compulsory flannel shirt and cap came and sat with us. "Drink?"

Before we knew it, they had submerged us into their group. As we swapped stories, excitement bubbled rapidly, like a witch's potion at boiling point.

"So, listen to this," Lochie a rosy-cheeked bearded surfer caught the attention of the group, "We've just come across from France, right, and one night a few of us went out late for some drinks and I only got my bloody phone nicked."

"No! How annoying," my mind wandered to the aspiring thieves we witnessed, could it be?

"All my photos from the trip, my way of talking to folks back home suddenly gone, right?" He looked around attempting to create suspense, I suspecting we were the only ones who didn't already know the ending. Although he was trying to tell us a somewhat sad story, I could help but smile at his accent.

"But then, my old girl back home gets a message from my phone!"

Ev laughed at Lochie's over the top dramatics; this man was the embodiment of every story he had told me about Australia.

"Saying what?" I pushed him on. "And how did he get into your phone?"

"I don't have a password, never needed one before. Only bloody asking for some ransom money for the phone back. Send three hundred euros and we'll post the fucken' phone!"

If this was the thieves we'd seen they'd definitely upped their game.

"Tell them what ya did Lochie," A woman with long golden hair called over.

"Ah nah," He smiled, clearly that wasn't the end.

The golden-haired woman came to join us, "He got his mum to message back, right, and say I need the phone or whatever and really lay it on, and ended with if you meet me I'll give ya five hundred euros."

"This isn't real, surely." Ev was invested.

"Sure is mate," Lochie smiled. "Long story short, we convinced this guy to meet me not far from where I'd been out the night before. Fucken' idiot thought he was gonna get five hundred euros, so he shows up, sends a little message to my mum and then waits. I watched him for a bit, then went over and offered him a stubby."

By this point I had many, *many*, questions but decided to stay quiet and just listen, true or not he had the audience captivated.

"Then what?" Ev asked after sinking a tequila shot that had arrived in front of him.

"Well then," He rubbed his chin and looked off to the right, "I smacked him between the eyes and nicked my phone back! Fucken' bogan."

The crowd erupted. Lochie looked smug and then darted inside before anyone could ask any questions. I didn't believe him, but I liked him so what was the harm in buying into his entertainment.

His drama sparked others to share theirs and in turn we shared just some of the chaos we'd experienced so far, all the while sinking more and more drinks.

Soon enough, we were onwards to the pub. A huge swarm of us patrolling through this charming, unobtrusive, rural community like villagers on a rampage, minus the rage and the pitchforks. We overfilled the low-ceilinged local's pub and turned what I imagine was a peaceful evening into a sound storm, in which it was very hard to move.

Whilst outside one of the Aussie lads yelled to Ev, "Oi look at your bird- shooting a dart and sculling a schooner!" Thankfully, Ev knew exactly what he meant and assured me it was not offensive and actually he was impressed by my *"laddish"* behaviour. Not wanting to get into a debate about what makes it "laddish" I necked another beer to soothe my pulsing face and took it as a compliment.

After a while, four of us, Ev, me, Bill, and Lochie, staggered away from the crowd. Yelling and laughing as we went, we scaled the outdoor staircase and tried very hard to get into the "members-only club" located above the pub. The staff inside were extremely hesitant, seeing as the room was rather small and already had a few local old men drinking within it. I understood the caution.

In that annoying-drunk-persistent-nagging way, we took turns trying to convince them why they should let us in, no argument any better than the last. In the end we were reduced to helpless pleading. It became a forbidden fruit situation. We could see the entire room. It was completely lifeless, so much so that tumbleweed wouldn't have been out of place, yet we were relentless. The more they said no, the more we wanted in. Finally, they agreed, or more likely gave in, and granted us access.

I was the only female in the room, and we were younger than all the other roisters by at least forty years, so *surprisingly*, the atmosphere was not great. In an attempt to add some life, we ordered a couple rounds of shots, offered them around, (to which we were met with raised eyebrows and disapproving head shakes) then howled like hooligans and wretched more and more dramatically as we sunk each tiny glass of potency. We were clearly having too much fun and made the tiresome staff regret their decision to let us in, thus promptly kicking us out again. Now steaming drunk, we all laid strewn on the pebbly ground outside admiring the unobstructed view of the stars and listened to the gently flowing waterfall beside us.

We shared stories for a long time. They told us about camping trips in the outback (they too loved a ridiculous camping accessory) and more about their present trip around Europe, whilst we shared more of the disasters and delights that we had experienced so far and where we were headed next.

After a long peaceful moment, we noticed there was no longer a surge of voices and realised everyone else had gone home, so peacefully we too stumbled our way back.

Unexpected Treasure

Once again, we awoke to a flight change email. Clearly booking very cheap flights with little-known airlines wasn't serving us so well. Already feeling dreadful, heads pounding and stomachs sick, the unwelcomed news instantly intensified our hangovers.

Our new flight was six hours earlier meaning we needed to head to Bern that night, rather than the following morning, otherwise we'd have no chance of getting to the airport in time. The thought of rerouting and hurriedly navigating once again added great force to our stampeding heads.

This time without too much internet fuss I was able to book us a room in a central hostel and thankfully our current home was happy to refund our unused night, our dwindling funds were temporarily safe at least. So far, the change was surprisingly easy to adjust to, minus the waves of acidic nausea and cranium splitting internal thuds.

Leaving was bittersweet; I was disappointed to move on from this beautiful place a day early, but now was excited to see more of Switzerland with Ev. It's a place I frequented as a child visiting family, and subsequently, I had fallen in love with it. I knew how surprisingly comparative their bustling cosmopolitan world is to that of other European countries.

Plus en-route to the city we would venture through more idyllic countryside where I could reminisce about the adventures we'd had when I was little. Carrying fire torches through the star-lit forest to a secret mountain shack for a cheesy feast, days spent swimming in Lake Geneva, delighting in waist-high snow one day and sunbathing the next, and my short time attending a Swiss school.

A place away from home has never felt so homely to me, the ease of access to nature and their methodical way of living that just makes total sense. It's typical, the place I love the most is the most expensive to visit, I've always had champagne taste and lemonade money, so I suppose why would travelling be any different?

Speaking of money, this change of location would definitely cost us. I knew that to eat/drink/ simply exist in Bern, would cost a lot more than our updated pitiful daily allowance; our remaining money spread equally over the next thirteen days allowed us to spend just six euros a day. That would equate to one coffee in Bern. Consequently, we were going to hit the bottom of our wallets very soon. I decided to deal with that later, desperately hoping someone else would fix it or that somehow, we would wake up very rich and this inconvenient problem would cease to be.

After a groggy goodbye to our new friends and a scenic reminiscent train ride, we arrived at our next stop. The beer pain combined with my vicious sinus-oozing ensured our pharmacy hunt would not be forgotten this time.

At last I was able to buy something that promised well-needed relief so without wasting a second I guzzled the antibiotics unapologetically. Instantly that day's budget, and the following three's, were blown.

In full tourist mode, we lugged our over-packed bags around in disoriented circles, distantly admired a river that we "planned" to swim in and stopped for an overpriced coffee break (another two days' budgets gone) before finally finding our hostel. Its location was excellent, close to the city centre and not far from the "lazy river" as we were now calling it, due to the constantly moving stream and evident likeness to those at water parks. Thankfully, we checked in without a problem so once we'd dumped our stuff in our tiny room we headed down to the communal area.

It was uncomfortably quiet. Full of people, but no sound. Faces engrossed in books, laptops and phones not noticing one another's existence. We watched the zombies with their unbroken focus. Looking around the draining room and seeing the lack of life Ev turned to me, "River time?"

If I am completely honest, I didn't fully believe we would go in; I thought they'd be barriers or it would be too cold or some sensible someone would talk us out of it, but I played along anyway. "Let's go," I smiled.

We grabbed our industrial-thick waterproof bag from the Bag Of Wonders and raced our way back into the street and then down the ten-thousand steps (approximately) that lead to the Aare River.

The sight was spectacular; perfectly clear turquoise water sprinkled with hundreds-and-thousands of brightly coloured people, either bobbing along or sunbathing beside it. I was awestruck and, for once, very happy to have been proved wrong.

Instantly we were approached by a heavily moustached man in a speedos and sandals. Anywhere else I would have run a mile, but this is Switzerland, and the fashion is *questionable*.

"Ha-lo!" Moustache boomed.

I stared, not able to gather any words.

"Hello mate." Ev mustered.

"Is this your first time visiting the Aare River?" He spoke with military seriousness; it was unexpected from a barely clothed talking moustache.

"Yes, we were hoping to swim, I can't believe we actually can!" I let out some of my previously hidden reservations.

"Yes, you can swim!" He chortled, "Now, what you should do is walk down that way," he pointed behind us, "It's the opposite direction of the current. You can jump right in; it's cold. Then you can then glide back down. Just perfect." He looked around as proud as a lion in the pride lands.

Ev and I exchanged eager glances.

"But," He added cautiously, "Part of the river is forbidden! You must pull yourselves out on to the bank before you pass the *ne pas nager* (no swimming) signs." Wisdom shared the gatekeeper looked through us in search of new people to advise, then marched on purposefully.

His words had made me nervous. The water was moving very quickly, and I doubted my abilities to fight the current. What would happen if I didn't get out in time? I dared not wonder.

Conveniently, I had time to observe other people's exiting techniques as Ev rolled himself a fag and pulled out two beers from the bag.

Some people made it look so easy, swimming through the current like a knife in butter then climbing out effortlessly, emerging on the bank fresh and energised. Others, splashed desperately as they were relentlessly pushed on, then when they finally reached the bank they clung on desperately catching their breath before they dared tried to ascend the rocks. The latter seemed a more achievable aim for me.

My temporary concerns were forcefully silenced by a sudden overwhelming excitement (and beer) as now ready we ran as far as we could, shoved all our things into the waterproof bag, and leapt in. Neither of us had expected the sudden shock from temperature change, from scorching hot in the sunshine to being fully submerged in a glacier river. "Cold" had been an understatement. It took me a short while to regain control of my quivering limbs, but as soon as I did, I felt pure joy seep through me.

Completely content -freezing- but content, we laid on our backs and allowed ourselves to be carried along the river, floating like otters with our hands interlocked and with the bag containing our most important items bobbing freely between us.

Everywhere we looked, people were smiling and braving the jump in. The atmosphere was heart-warming, which made the water's icy grips a bit more bearable. Another unexpected treasure, and such uncomplicated fun within nature: something we can all benefit from more of.

Reality's harshness came back forcefully as Ev yelled, "Oh shit! There's the sign!" and we began our dash to the edge. As predicted, this was not a simple task. The water pushed us on as we tried to swim in line. Without too much of an issue, Ev pushed himself through the water and jumped out onto the bank. Once stable he turned and stretched an arm toward me, but it was too late, the current had snatched me away. It seemed my weedy arms were no match for the drift. I kept fighting, now with desperation fuelling my limbs, but still I managed to miss three more exit points.

I began contemplating what would be worse; the punishment for breaking the rules or the mystery lurking within the danger zone. Fear narrated my sudden wonder of what the restricted zone held, a sheer drop into frothy rapids? Shoals of starved piranhas? Scenes involving a lot of pain, and consequently death, rolled before my eyes as I inhaled more and more water. Thankfully, I was able to grab hold of the bank just before being forced to find out, only causing minor surface injuries as I dragged myself up the jagged rocks and onto still land where Ev awaited to console my worries and inflate my sunken ego.

The near-death experience wasn't enough to keep me waterside. Instead, we created a new method, in which we would keep our hands locked together for the duration of the drift and then Ev would pull me from the current before we got too far. We had noticed parents doing this with their infant children, I decided to ignore that part and my self-esteem thanked me. We repeated this process for hours, sometimes taking much longer walks against the current to enjoy extended water time, and other times just running a few steps then launching ourselves back in. It was so joyful, and again that childlike freedom absorbed us as we screamed and laughed and played without a care in the world. Thankfully, our (my) exit strategy improved, meaning we left there that evening feeling happy, exhausted and withholding only a couple of scrapes and bruises. The bag's waterproofness was mostly sufficient, everything came out a damp, sweaty wet but still in perfect working-tact.

Back at the hostel we cooked ourselves the gourmet meal of *supernoodles*, or at least the Swiss equivalent, this meal was definitely budget friendly. If only we hadn't already blown several more days' spends at a bar on our walk home.

Yet again the common room held a tense silence as people avoided one another so we went to bed ready for the extremely early flight to

Munich the next day. We planned our alternative route fastidiously, as everything else had strived to be, then settled for a few hours' sleep.

Gypsy Gutter

As morning had barely arrived, we slothfully gathered our things before making our way to a nearby bus-stop with the plans to catch a direct shuttle to the airport. Sounds easy, right?

However, upon reaching the bus-stop we found that there was no bus. The first bus wasn't for over an hour, which meant if we were to wait for it we would 1. Be very late for our flight and 2. We needn't have dragged ourselves so painfully out of bed at this ridiculous hour. Once again, the internet had misinformed us, or maybe we had failed to notice the daily change of schedule. Whatever the cause, we now had a big problem.

Trying to keep calm but feeling that all-too-familiar imminent time pressure, and knowing how the minutes would likely become seconds now that we were panicking, we pleaded for advice from anyone we saw. Most were people still out from the night before, many being fellow travellers, so obviously, provided little help. Each interaction with a friendly, sympathetic, or begrudged drunk just added to my certainty that we would definitely miss this flight. We had managed to find luck in the face of each disruption so far, but I couldn't see a way out. There's no positivity to be found, internally or externally, that early in the morning. No buses were running, taxis were non-existent, and the streets were swiftly emptying. As the city cleared, the eeriness of our previous lost-panic began creeping in. Unsure what else to do, we stood helplessly in a dusky daze, hoping for a saviour.

After at least thirty-accelerated-minutes of aimless panic-strolling, I spotted a man with a smart blazer jacket yielding no visible alcohol so without a second thought I accosted him.

"Hello! Hi! Good morning, we're trying to get to the airport, our flight leaves really soon - the bus didn't come, or isn't until later, and we don't know what to do, please can you help us?" I babbled at the unsuspecting victim.

"Oh hel-lo. No, no buses yet. But, the train station is now open, and there is a train to the airport in five minutes." He informed us.

One thing about Switzerland is that the trains are always, always, on time. So if it's scheduled to depart in five minutes, then it was most definitely going to depart in five minutes. We ran.

Both of us were full-on panic sprinting through an unfamiliar train station full of pure desperation. How better to begin the day?

Unnervingly easily we were able to buy tickets, and then settle ourselves onto the airport-heading-train with even a minute to spare. I looked around suspiciously, something wasn't right. It's never this easy.

More understandably, we then realised that this train was in fact heading to Zurich airport, rather than our desired destination of Bern airport.

Off we ran again just as the train doors shut. My skin felt the force of the doors shutting, if I had been wearing something slightly thicker, I would have been trapped in the door and dragged along with it. At least that way I'd have been on my way somewhere rather than just standing there so hopelessly. More time and money wasted, and we were still no closer to our destination.

Time was disappearing. I was worried that we wouldn't get through customs in time, or they would start boarding before we arrived, and that we would end up missing the flight. Previously my family and I had arrived too late for a flight, after we first went to the wrong airport (clearly, I am not the only calamity,) and Ev and I did not have the extortionate funds that thankfully my dad did that day for last-minute flights. Missing the flight would leave us stranded. And in Switzerland, of all money-draining places.

So far the trip was not what I had expected: two young nomads lovingly weaving between countries with loaded backpacks and peaceful minds. Instead, it was mad-rushed hungover wayward morons failing to navigate the internet's abundance of information or, apparently, any form of public transport. Travelling was hard and stressful.

But, in spite of all the panic we had laughed -a lot. Our relationship was being tested, stretched, spun, spat at and pulled apart to within an inch of its life in a wildly intense environment, but yet we laughed all day every day. Maybe not all day, but definitely every day. Plus, we doted on one another throughout. Silly gifts from shops we couldn't afford to be in, that extra beer at the end of the night when we should really go to sleep, tight hugs in the morning. That kept us going and allowed us to easily forgive the stressed-out snaps at each other and the endless blame game. It was, of course, all my fault.

Another official-looking person, by official I mean not drunk and this time wearing a high-vis, spotted our distress and pointed us in the direction of the shuttle bus we had sought after in the first place. We had spent so much time achieving nothing, the later bus was now here. Without a quicker option, we boarded the bus and desperately hoped we still had enough time. Still the sun had not risen, and we had experienced enough stress and panic to last a week, all on uncomfortably empty stomachs.

Now Time slowed down. Apprehension of what would happen at the airport built and built until I had convinced myself that not only would they refuse us to board but they would also scream and shout at us and then arrest us, and bar us unorganised messes from ever returning to their perfectly efficient country. My mind raced as the bus dawdled.

After what felt like decades on the silent bus, we arrived at the airport. We and two others departed to make our way in.

I was shocked to see such emptiness, quiet, not a queue in sight. The total opposite to the mad panic that airports normally emulate, and that of our morning thus far. The airport was tiny; we could see each end of the building from where we stood. It would have taken a mere few minutes to walk the perimeter.

After no time at all, we were through customs, checked-in, and ready to board, with time to spare for extortionately expensive croissants and coffee! It was by far the easiest airport experience I have ever had. Panic over.

Not too long after, our plane arrived. It was tiny. From the distance of the airport, it looked like a collector's figurine. A private plane just for us? Surely not. Our names were called, we stepped forward and awaited other names to follow. Nope. Just us.

Feeling like VIPs we followed a steward across the hanger and boarded our personal plane. This day kept getting weirder.

There were only nine passenger seats on board: two seats on the right aisle and one on the left, with just three rows going back. Those few seats weren't even full; it really was just for us.

So bizarre, maybe they thought we were some fancy Brits on an opulent globe-trotting through Europe, not the two over-planned, under-organised idiots bumbling between countries.

After take-off, the crew delivered us some seemingly homemade sandwiches wrapped up in tinfoil, plus a banana and a slice of cake each. It felt like I was back at primary school and opening my packed lunch box to see what treats my mum had made. This tranquillity, compared to the usual discomfort of flying, felt so surreal but was completely favourable - no wonder private jets are the utmost luxury way to travel, this was heavenly.

Since then, the only flight that has even slightly compared was when we were travelling to Majorca shortly after the borders reopened, post-pandemic. We were a group of eight, four adults and four children, and it couldn't have been easier due to the reduced flights and minimal travellers. Life's so much calmer without the overbearing crowds filled with hotheads and personal-space-invaders ruining everything, alas we're far from millionaires so we'll just enjoy these comforts when they arise and accept that stressed out irritating people are just a part of the journey.

Unlike the start of the day, we landed, left Munich airport and made it into the city without difficulty. Knowing how fragile these problem free times were, we decided to spend a few hours exploring slowly, instead of rushing on to our next destination. We drank coffee in the sun and ate everything in sight.

Now came the time to face the overhanging issue I had been ignoring. The money was gone. I hadn't *got rich quick*, or woken up to a huge not-played-lottery win, or been rescued by an all seeing presence. We had just spent the last of the money on our third coffee since arriving in the city. We were at peace but completely penniless. I bit the bullet,

"We've run out of money." I briskly told Ev. I assumed he was aware but thought best that we actually discuss our new bankruptcy.

He chuffed his fag, swigged his coffee and looked back at me with a devilish grin.

I knew what he was thinking, "What?" I probed anyway.

"We could use your credit card, try not to spend too much and then we'll pay it off when we get home. We'll split it; I doubt we'll spend loads anyway." Did he even believe the words as they left his mouth?

"Mmmm," I searched the air one last time for another option; I knew we would spend a lot and I knew we would put off paying it back so it was a less than desirable plan. With no alternatives making themselves known I agreed, regrettably, that the time had come to start using my "emergency" credit card.

With a swift peel of a sticker, it was ready to use, and our funds went soaring up again. Thankfully, it only had a one-thousand-five-hundred-pound limit so that would be the *absolute most* we could squander.

Sensibly we agreed that we wouldn't need that much, seeing as it was almost double what we had actually bought with us. We reasoned another fifty euros would suffice for the day then for the following eleven days we would return to that long-lost forty euros per day idea, leaving me more than enough left for real emergencies when I returned to uni. Great plan. Achievable? Absolutely not.

We were spending the next two nights in Ohlstadt, which was about an hour away from Munich on the train. No need to rush, let's just enjoy not having to gather coins and rejoice in the lack of panic for a while, or so we thought.

After leisurely wandering around the historical city, we felt calm again and eager to enjoy the rest of the day. Comparatively, our arrival at our next temporary home was an intense sensory overload, the kind of thing you need to process in slow motion.

Firstly, I'll explain where we were staying. I had found something that appealed to my inner hippy, a converted trailer with a rainwater shower, eco toilet (not knowing what this was), central fire pit and totally surrounded by fields occupied by wild horses. Sounds like a cool bohemian retreat? I thought so, and was *so* excited for this stop, but of course things are not always what they seem.

Following a twenty-minute hot and sticky walk from the train station (thankfully google maps was on our side this time) we made our way up a vast dirt track to arrive at the hippy haven.

Instantly our eyes were drawn to a young woman, who was dripping wet wearing only a crispy brown towel and covered in huge red lumps. She was standing all alone sobbing enormous, animated tears like that of a cartoon. I could literally see the fountain of tears billowing out of her swollen eyes.

Before I could say anything to her, an angry German woman intercepted as she stormed towards us, accompanied by a drooling grey dog nearly as tall as me. Her fierce stomps and oversized work boots made her appear like a rampaging giant. Immediately she began bellowing, "You're late! You should have been here hours ago. Check in opened from two and it is now six o'clock!" *From two* clearly being the phrase that caused confusion in translation.

We apologised, unnecessarily but trying to avoid conflict, and she begrudgingly showed us to our "room".

The crying woman was still standing there sobbing to herself, each one of my concerned looks in her direction was deflected by a dismissive glare from the terrifying owner.

As we walked, an intense farm-like smell entered my clearing nose. Having spent hours playing amongst my family's farm I thought I would be used to animal scents- or at least not hypersensitive to them, but this was different and pungently eye-watering even through the, now thinning, cheese-sauce that was still lingering painfully in my nose. It wasn't until hours later that I worked out what this foul odour was.

Instantly it was clear that our room was a lot less flower-power-vogue than I had imagined; the hot tin container was full of spiders, years of undisturbed dust and a suffocating smell of damp. Plus, there was just one single bed!

"There is another mattress under the bed, pull it out and one of you can lay on the floor." The owner barked at us.

It's rare that even Ev is stunned silent but we both just gawped at her. Our lack of response was enough to encourage her to leave, she stomped back out leaving us alone in the filth.

"What. The. Fuck?" I looked at Ev, my heartrate accelerating by the second.

He grabbed my hand to lead me back out of the pungent room, "It's not that bad," he lied.

"It is." I exhaled deeply.

"Okay it is. But don't panic. It will be okay; we need to go and get food and maybe when we get back it won't be so bad."

"It won't be okay. It stinks, and it's dirty and she's mean!" I was whispering violently so she didn't overhear and reprimand me.

There was nothing Ev could say to pause the panic at this point, my head was gone. Instead, he went to enquire about where we could buy some food.

This enraged the woman even more. Bitterly she informed him that there wasn't anywhere in walking distance that would be open. She grumbled, "You will have to come in the car with me, but we are stopping at the hospital first. We go now, hurry up and be ready."

I do not envy Ev who then had to come and relay this to me whilst I was in a full-on princess panic about this vile setting.

"I don't want to do that either, but we don't have another option!" He tried to remain calm as I sulked, "I could go, and you wait here?"

"Do not leave me here!" I jumped to attention.

"Well let's go then, we don't want to piss her off anymore."

So that was that. Just minutes after arriving we were off again. Ev, me, the crying naked woman, her boyfriend (who had now appeared?), the angry lady, and the big dribbling dog, all loaded into the grottiest car I have ever seen.

The seats were thick with dried dog saliva and an entire universe existed in the filth on the floor. I sat perched on the very edge of my seat, trying not to let my skin touch anything. All the while, the dog hung his head over from the boot and blew his hot, squalid breath in my face. The crying woman's boyfriend explained that something had bitten her in their trailer whilst they were asleep the previous night, and it had become more inflamed throughout the day. Obviously, this made us feel even better about our stay in this dirty dump land.

After an extremely uncomfortable half an hour of small-talk, sobs, and stares, we arrived at the hospital. The three of them went in whilst we stayed in the car with the dog. I was pleased the medicine I had purchased had started my own recovery, as I didn't fancy the idea of going in alongside them. I remember so clearly looking at Ev full of desperation and him looking back much the same.

We had no idea how long we were going to be waiting, or really what was going on, so just sat there trying to keep the increasingly restless dog occupied. His low rumbling growls flicked saliva all over the dungy car whilst his crazed eyes stayed fixed on me. The longer we waited in this rapidly heating vehicle, the more stomping and scratching he proceeded to do.

"This dog is going to kill me." I had made peace with it.

Normally one to brush off my panic or talk down my fears Ev couldn't help but agree, "He doesn't seem to like you much."

"I don't particularly like him either." With that, the malevolent beast snapped his gnashers at me.

How had this happened?

Just hours ago we had been loving life while drinking copious amounts of caffeine (which perhaps wasn't helping me remain calm?) in Munich and now we were trapped in a well-hidden gypsy gutter.

After far too long, the angry lady reappeared,

"They will return later on," She explained nonchalantly, "Now we can go to the supermarket."

We nodded obediently.

I was pleased she had returned but annoyed she had left us in charge of her demon dog with no care instructions, for what felt like hours. I kept that annoyance silent. On reflection, that was one of my few good decisions.

Once we arrived at the shop, we leaped out of the car and the German Giantess called to us, "Don't be late!" whilst cackling horrifically.

We were sure to move fast to avoid abandonment, grabbing an abundance of beer and easy to cook food - at the site, we had noticed an evident lack of kitchen as promised (or imagined, I'm uncertain), more a makeshift canopy over hazardous looking outdoor hobs.

The drive back was a bit more pleasant. Her anger seemed to have dwindled. She explained we could use whatever kitchen utensils we could find as long as we washed them, this was said with sergeant-like meaning. She then suggested setting up a fire that evening if we fancied it, and even offered for us to borrow two of her bikes the following day if we wanted to cycle to the "beautiful lake" nearby.

The giantess' mood had shifted so dramatically that it was unsettling. I felt like I was being trapped or coerced and soon she would attempt to keep us as permanent prisoners. There would be no Stockholm syndrome here. I hated her- her unnecessary anger, smelly house and evil dog had assured that.

Pulling back up to the murderous-farm-setting, the dread of sleeping in the dirty spider filled tin-can was taking over. I could barely convince myself to step back inside it, so how was I supposed to last two whole nights in there?

My mood eased a little when I saw a few other guests, none that were covered in red bites or sobbing. Together we sat and drank beers around the quickly assembled fire. I almost relaxed, until I needed the toilet, that was.

Picture a porta-loo, without a light and full of spiders. But of course, it was an "eco-toilet," and now was the time I found out what that meant: a glorified hole in the ground, beneath a toilet seat, where human waste is left to "compost". So that was the sour smell that had welcomed us, I concluded.

I was nearly sick just by opening the door. The odour burned into my nostrils, the putrid smell now not at all dulled by my infectious ooze. I decided a nearby bush would suffice for the duration of the stay.

Feeling a bit beer-brave we decided we may as well attempt all the amenities and made for the shower. Bizarrely (or by now maybe nothing should be?) it was situated within the communal "kitchen" with just a short rickety door that barely covered our middle sections, (due to everywhere else's spider abundance I insisted that Ev and I go in together).

It was exactly as advertised, a rainwater shower. Rain had fallen into a large plastic bin and we scooped it up with a grotty jug and showered it over one another whilst gasping with cold water shock, much to the amusement of everyone around who had a clear sight of our faces and curling toes. It wasn't dissimilar to the portable camping shower we had been lugging around and opted not to use. There had *always* been a better option, until now. I had well and truly romanticised this place rather than reading the description logically.

Not particularly clean, we scampered to our room to change. This was extremely difficult as I constantly twitched at the thought of spiders, and other hidden monsters, crawling over my exposed skin. Any hints of cleanliness were quickly replaced with the thick damp air that swamped into our pores. Pure luxury.

As quickly as possible, we hurtled back out of the aluminium vessel, panting for fresh oxygen, already smelling worse than before the shower. The musky aroma clung to us like lycra in the rain.

We were eager to cook so we could then spend the rest of the evening sitting around the fire drinking away our present worries. The earlier instruction for us to wash all the kitchen utensils had falsely led me to believe that we would be cooking in a clean space that night. Trying our best to ignore the layers upon layers of filth, we made sure to scrub everything before we used it. We are not clean enthusiasts in our own home by any stretch and can comfortably ignore a lot more mess than most, but this was really rough. Thick burnt sticky substances coated each utensil so firmly thus confirming it was age old grim. At least each aspect of this angry woman's home was consistent, filthy, dank and sticky, but consistent. She demonstrated a true individual style.

Unfortunately, the hygienic illusion we were trying to create was shattered when the owner herself pulled a spoon from the drawer, scooped out sloppy brown dog food from an already open and fly-infested tin, rubbed it "clean" with her thumb and then placed it back in the drawer. Surprisingly, my appetite diminished. This time even Ev was put off. Not wanting to touch anything further we dined on sparsely cooked pasta and poured over a cold jar of sauce. Evidently it wasn't the worst thing I've ever cooked. At least the beers couldn't be dirtied.

Food forced down, we retired to the fire. I was just beginning to ease up when the couple from our earlier car ride returned. The crying woman was much happier (no longer crying) . She explained that the doctor had given her antibiotics for the monstrous bed bites, and all would be fine, so they were going to continue their stay(!!).

Apparently, they were frequent visitors and something like this wouldn't put them off, the Stockholm syndrome had got a hold of them it seemed. I smiled encouragingly, but my head was definitely objecting. I thought of our previous abodes, and the dramas they had brought, but still I would have preferred any one of them over this place.

That night I went to bed with every inch of my skin covered, I'd have rather boiled than let any part of that room touch me. Uncomfortable, hot and sweating we both squished onto the single bed as I couldn't bear being "alone" in case a creepy crawly or a dirt monster came too close.

Plus, I dreaded to think what the under-bed mattress would bring out with it. Another billion lifetimes of dirt, huge crawlies, the corpse of the last visitor? For the first time on the trip I felt unquestionably desperate to leave somewhere.

I laid awake worrying for a while, until Ev let out a hefty reflective sigh.

I lifted my head from his chest to face him.

"This trip has been weird." He smiled followed by a stifled laugh, he'd opted for a kinder adjective than necessary.

I returned the smile apologetically, I'd really tried and hoped he knew that.

We both erupted in enigmatic laughter until at last we lay lightly in shallow sleep.

Bare Bummed Squatting

It was a restless night, punctuated with an unnecessary amount of anxious-wees in the bushes. As the sun had barely risen, we found ourselves engulfed in hot flushes so frantically piled out of the tin-can. My clothes were stuck to me with a gluey sweat, so I reluctantly faced the rainwater shower again (and again forced Ev to accompany me).

As promised, we were lent two bikes so that we could explore our sparse surroundings and, most importantly, find the "beautiful lake." Following a gourmet breakfast of tomato and butter sandwiches (anything to avoid use of the "kitchen") we received some vague instructions that I did not listen to, and then set off soaring down the wide country roads. I paid no attention to where we were going, or where we had come from, just enjoyed the uncultivated scenery. As we were so remote, we hardly saw another person for almost an hour.

In pure joy, we coasted down winding roads framed with towering green trees, feeling free and happy to be away from other people for a while. Time to just be us again.

However, before long, we were extremely hot, completely lost and painfully thirsty. So incredibly thirsty. When taking a short pause to cool down, we suddenly became very aware of *how* alone we were. This realisation enhanced the ominous lost feeling quite drastically, so we set off promptly in search of other life forms, and water. Again, echoes of France were cascading around my head, and I so hoped this time we would come across some more friendly locals; it seemed I had fresh but significant scars as each hint of being lost mentally transported me back to our most helpless state.

After months of pedalling, we found a very still, quiet village. Being surrounded by houses, rather than endless trees and fields, made us hopeful that we would soon find someone who could help us find our way to the lake.

We cycled on, still without any sign that there was anyone else in the world. We cycled on, there were still no people but, we were pleased to find an ancient water pump. We took turns sticking our heads underneath it and chaotically pumped water all over each other's thirsty faces. One problem was solved at least.

As if we'd timed it, a man now zoomed past us on a racing bike. He was the real deal, a speed demon on a lightweight bike, wearing luminous lyra, a stupidly long helmet, and hideous orange glasses that looked more like science goggles than sun protectors.

Desperately, we called out after him, pleading for help. Reluctantly he stopped, swiftly turning his bike then staring at us expectantly. Ev relayed the information we were given that morning whilst I perused him, desperately searching for a clue as to why anyone would ever partake in this muscle-aching road-raging hobby.

The man understood the vague directions better than Ev had and quickly worked out where we were headed. As if it pained him to do so, he agreed to show us the way to the lake. For the most part, we could just follow him as, as luck would have it, he was heading in the same direction. This act of true kindness came with just one strict condition, "You must keep to my speed. If you do not, and you fall behind, I will not wait. So you pedal quickly, okay?" He was a MAMIL (middle aged man in lycra) hopelessly devoted to his own cause, and we would not stand in his way.

Feeling like naughty school children who'd had the rules enforced, we nodded awkwardly without another choice. Our chase started with good intentions, and with *a lot* of effort we could just about keep up.

However, we soon came to a scarily steep incline. Wordlessly we were both in agreement that I had no chance of scaling it whilst maintaining this racy pace. Our last hope was for Ev to cycle ahead until the MAMIL was no longer on our route, obtain the remaining directions, then come back for me as I leisurely conquered the vertical mound.

Trying not to feel like an unfit, incapable burden I watched them soar high into the clouds as I panted and puffed my way along.

This plan worked well for all of about six minutes, before Ev returned to me drenched with sweat and gasping for air only to explain that he too had lost the man. Wonderful.

Without a lot of panic, we were too hot and tired to use any more energy; we reasoned we must be close to the destination as we had been cycling for so long. No evidence supported our thoughts, but they kept us going. Foolishly, we dreamt aloud of water, ice-creams and cold beers whilst our delirious heads created teasing mirages.

Somehow, after many more wrong turns, we arrived. It turned out this is where everyone, and their dogs, cats, hamsters, and pigeons, had been all day; It was hideously over-populated.

My crowd-avoidant self immediately wanted to leave, but now in desperate need of hydration I overcame my *Need To Retreat* and instead found a café and got in line. I had never been so desperate for a drink.

In a soul-crushing moment, it was now we realised that neither one of us had brought any form of money. Each one thinking the other had. What made this even more infuriating is that we had done the exact same thing a few months prior on a budget-break to Turkey. (That one really was budget. We had booked and paid for the entire two weeks after a lucky two-hundred-and-fifty-pound scratch card win. Two hundred and fifty pounds is a great win, but for an entire two week holiday? You can imagine the place we ended up in.)

This trip, however, had taught us a lot, but the best thing was that this would never happen to Ev again. These unorganised messes still happen to me on a weekly basis, but he knows that if he isn't on-the-ball we'll be hungry, lost or stranded. One day maybe I'll stop being a forgetful calamitous, but I can't see much chance of change on the coming horizon.

Scraping our sunken hearts from the floor, we looked around for a solution. Our only option was to go into the public toilets and drink from the sink, far from ideal (nor classy), but it would have to do as we so needed liquid. I could feel my insides turning more and more raisin-like by the second.

The only thing that stood in our way was the gruesome toilet guard demanding fifty cents per person to enter, which, obviously, we didn't have. Thinking quickly, I served as a distraction, "Hello - sir, how are you today?"

The overweight man in the yellow stained vest just stared at me.

I felt my awkward shoulders shifting upwards, " I was just wondering, do you know where the lake is? We've been cycling for hours and we're not from around here, as you can tell I'm not German but we've been looking for the lake and um-"

Whilst I babbled Ev snuck behind the toilet guard. Over the guard's shoulder I saw him slyly reach into the plastic tub snatch and handful of fifty cent coins.

"-we're very lost, so could you help me?" I finally brought my nervous diversion to a close.

Without so much as a facial twitch he extended his index finger towards me.

In pretend shock I turned around and then back to him with a would-you-believe-it gesticulation and a wide smile.

Still no emotion from the guard.

Ev was now back at my side and casually handed me a fifty-cent coin to which I pleasantly threw back into the tub, therefore gaining access to the grimy watering hole.

Through all the excitement of hydrating ourselves, we had failed to truly take in the sight of the lake that we had tried so hard to find. It was exceptionally underwhelming; a glorified murky pond surrounded by herds of loud people.

We sat down and tried to enjoy the attraction. However our view of said pond was blocked by an unavoidable obstruction: two excessively overweight people dry humping vigorously just metres in front of us. Not quite the fairytale setting I had imagined.

With the aim of adding entertainment I bombarded Ev's withering mind with more nonsensical questions,

"Would you rather have eyes on the end of your fingers, or fingers around the edge of your eyes?"

"Would you rather be seen and not heard, or heard and not seen?" The latter already being somewhat true for Ev and his carrying voice.

After a while of not enjoying our surroundings, but also not wanting to attempt to cycle back (combined with Ev's desperation for me to stop asking questions) we got to the point where the tepid tap water wasn't cutting it. Bodies aching, and feeling completely fed up, we forced ourselves back onto the bikes in search of home and real hydration/booze. For once we weren't thinking about food; we knew food meant cooking, and cooking meant that reentering that sticky kitchen.

Our return journey was a lot less stressful; Ev felt confident he could navigate us back and as always, I blindly followed. En-route, we passed by an exquisitely clear glacial lake (we definitely didn't come this way, but I wasn't in a position to question his navigation). It was free flowing from a distant waterfall and held panoramic views of the framing mountains and undistributed countryside. Yet, it was completely empty? Why was this not the hotspot? I suppose the lack of fast food, and flat ground to hump on, meant this natural beauty wasn't as appealing to the masses.

Obviously, we stopped and instantly attempted to splash around in the icy water. The stream ran fast over smoothed pebbles; the water was so cold it bit viciously at my toes as I went to step in. So, instead, I took to just letting the water gently lap over my feet when it dared to edge further up the stoney shore.

After a few minutes, I noticed Ev staring at me with an uncomfortable expression. He looked like a toddler too shy to say hello. I looked around fearfully, but when I found no answers, I returned the look quizzically.

"I need to poo." He announced, "Right now."

"Okay?" I wasn't sure what I was supposed to do with that information.

"I'm going to do it in the lake, then it will be swept away." He looked at me for input.

"To be honest, it's better than that hell hole eco-toilet." Weird, and often gross, things happen when I'm with Ev, but I hadn't expected we'd be in a situation in which we'd be discussing the whereabouts for his pooing needs on our lovers' holiday.

"You need to keep guard." He instructed as he began wading through the freezing water. "Let me know if anyone comes."

How romantic, I thought.

Unfortunately, I found the sight of him stone-walking through the frosty water, and then bare bummed squatting into it, too hilarious to do any guarding whatsoever. When it was far too late, I noticed a family overlooking the lake, in utter disgust, from a perfectly slanted hill opposite us. This only made it more amusing for me, but obviously not so much for Ev. Safe to say he was less than pleased with my guard keeping. At least I didn't charge fifty cents.

Mission accomplished, he stomped past me, his toes a bitter shade of blue.

When we finally arrived back that evening, we were so hungry and thirsty that we ate and drank everything we had left (that didn't require any use of kitchen tools whatsoever- raw carrots and tomatoes with a side of crisps so spicy my tongue felt like it had been attacked with a million needles, and a crate of beer it was), plus a few extra beers from the owner's "off limits" fridge, as payback for overselling and under-directing us to that crowded swamp land. Once drunk, I anxiously awaited her fretful roars, but thankfully, they never came.

We spent another night around the campfire, this time with a young German couple. We all chatted until the early hours of the morning. Their interest in language was fascinating. They knew more about the words in our native tongue than we did, and both of them were aiming to be speech therapists in England in the near future. They discussed how the importance of learning English is paramount in their schooling system and I felt embarrassed to say that, from my experience, as a pupil and as a soon-to-be-teacher, that languages weren't given the same value in our education system. They are touched upon, but the unsaid understanding that other people will understand us creates a hard to break barrier to the hard work needed to learn a language.

That night we went to bed much more easily; the combination of exhaustion, beer and the promise of tomorrow's luxury apartment in Vienna lured us to sleep. One more night of discomfort and then an entire apartment to ourselves to recharge, relax, and rest. Luxury, comfort, and basic cleanliness had never been so appealing.

Unfortunately, that wasn't what greeted us. Obviously.

IDIOTIC DENIAL

After another hot and scary night, morning was welcomed eagerly. Although I had accidentally set the alarms for the PM, *again*, we awoke in a timely fashion. Quickly, we gathered our stuff and for the first time felt truly pleased to be leaving somewhere.

In no time at all, we had left the revolting "hippy" camp behind us and were waiting to catch a train back into Munich, where we would get a lift to Vienna.

I had booked us a lift through a ride-sharing website, something neither of us had done before or known anyone else to do, but it was much cheaper than the train and that was enough to lure me in. Our driver was a German man named Peter. We had his registration number, and that was all we knew. Before that morning that had seemed like enough but stood awaiting his arrival my ever-waiting worries reared their ugly heads.

Promptly at eleven o'clock, we got to our agreed meeting point and realised we were totally unsure of what to expect for the upcoming four-hour car journey. The sudden fear that he wouldn't show up loomed over me, and then a worse one followed: that he would abduct and/or kill us. My dramatic narratives were fleeting once more.

Thankfully, Peter pulled up in his old blue Honda and seemed pleasant enough so without any more hesitations we hopped in. He explained that we should sit in the back as someone else had already booked the front seat. This suited us just fine as it removed that awkward forced car chat that often comes with taxi rides, I supposed we couldn't exactly ask him if he'd been busy or what time he finished.

Peter remained outside of the vehicle, awaiting his other passenger. I watched him through the window, weighing up how much of a potential threat he was. He was average height with a lanky build and a slightly hunched posture (otherwise known as nerd neck) from what I assumed was many hours on the computer. He was wearing thick rimmed glasses and an overworn Star Wars T-shirt. Trying not to make rash judgements on appearances alone I felt comfortable in his presence, and at worst I was confident Ev could "take him" if he became murderous.

After a few minutes, a round man full of energy bounded up to the car and after a quick introduction, they both jumped in. As the rattly engine came to life the stereo picked up where it had left off, Green Day's *American Idiot* blasted out. Peter's cheeks flushed red as his hand shot to turn the volume down.

Minutes into the journey, Peter announced, "My sister thinks it is so very ridiculous that I am driving this car so far. It is very old. She thinks I won't make it." He followed this harrowing announcement with a quiet chuckle.

This was really reassuring, as we were being driven to another country by a total stranger. I looked at Ev, eyes wide and my sky-high eyebrows causing deep furrows on my forehead. With every wheeze of the engine, I felt my jaw tighten. This trip was ageing me.

Michael, the other passenger, was *very* excited.

"I am travelling to Vienna to find out about my ancestors;" he shared without any prompting. "I have spent months and months tracing my family history, and now it is leading me out of Germany and into Vienna. How exciting! I am going to see if I can find some distant relatives. I have many questions about my grandparents and maybe someone can help me." He spoke of this with the energy of an animated children's TV presenter whilst we tried to mirror his excitement supportively, *oooohing* and nodding along.

After about an hour of us getting to know one another on a surface level (jobs, travel plans, relationships), they naturally fell back to German and spoke between themselves, leaving us to take in the sights and relax. As a way to channel my anxious energy I had begun writing a fictional novel (yet to be completed), so spent the duration typing away on my iPad, ready to read to Ev that night as per our new routine.

What could have been an awkward, or even deadly, trip was actually one of the easiest journeys we had and far more convenient than train-hopping with our ridiculous amount of stuff (waterless toothbrushes, umbrella hats, clip-to-collar fans (that did not work)). It was almost like having a private chauffeur, minus the fully functioning car and fancy hat.

The journey passed seamlessly and soon enough we were at the train station in Vienna feeling very confused about where we were supposed to be going and how to buy a ticket.

Nobody wanted to help us, and our overall existence seemed to annoy everyone who saw us, but, for once, I didn't care. Rejuvenation from leaving that awful tin-can and the excitement for our own apartment, combined with the relief that Peter's car did survive the journey, had completely lifted my spirits and grumpy people were not going to overthrow them. We were so close to our mid-trip luxury: an actual toilet, a hot shower, a proper bed, oven, washing machine- everything we needed, and more!

Finally, we sussed the train system. We hopped on board for a brief journey, just out of town (we hoped), to find our apartment.

Unfortunately, our excitement quivered a considerable amount when we deboarded.

We had unintentionally found *that* part of the city, the part you aren't meant to see. Every city has it, a rundown town that isn't designed for tourists, and consequently, you are not particularly welcome. The colours don't seem as vivid, the faces are unhappy, and the shops sell weird sexual things. Feeling certain this murkiness would just surround the station, we smiled falsely at each other and hurried in the direction of the address hanging out of my, now battered, folder.

The town got bleaker the further we walked, as if the leaving train on its escape to better places was sucking all the colour away with it. As we walked further into this sullen suburb, we came closer to our destination. However, as we approached it, we encountered an issue.

The building was not there, well, not fully there at least. We paced frantically up and down, trying to convince ourselves that we must have been making a mistake, even though the address was clearly for this partly torn-down building. The one that was currently in the process of being carelessly demolished right before our disappointed eyes.

"It can't be that one, let's walk on a bit further." I pleaded with the universe for help.

"We can't just walk around aimlessly; we need to find the apartment." Ev noted a flaw in my plan.

"Well, it can't be here so let's keep walking." I tried again to run from the problem.

He stared at me, his feet rooted to the floor, "It's here." He gestured towards an active destruction site.

"Surely not." I huffed as my shoulders slid to the floor, my hopeful yet idiotic denial hadn't been enough to make our newest drama disappear.

"This is the address, have you got a code for the gate?" He was stone serious, a rarity. Things were really bad.

I flicked through the folder each page reminding me of a previous problem, (deceptively remote, terrifying, at the top of a colossal mountain, sickeningly filthy) but at least they had all been whole and as ungracious as they were, they all expected us, it seemed here we must have been forgotten.

I found the code. Looking up at Ev I nodded and read it aloud.

Tentatively he punched it in, and of course, the metal gates began to open. For the first time I wished our search had been longer and less successful.

Hesitantly, we walked through the building site, the builders were just as surprised to see us as we were to see them, my suspicions were confirmed we had been forgotten.

What was once a grand apartment block was now a sea of rubble.

"Ev, what are we doing? We clearly can't stay here!" I flapped as the men around watched our every move.

"Come on." He instructed. His sudden sternness made him almost unfamiliar. Desperate not to give up, he led me towards a part of the building still relatively whole. "In here?"

I shrugged. The last thing I wanted to do was enter that building but I suspected that was exactly what was about to happen. Again, my suspicions were confirmed. This sudden foresight had arrived just a tad too late.

Without another choice, I followed him inside and we began climbing the spiral staircase, cautious not to fall through it. The overpowering crashes of a jackhammer shattering the remaining stone pillars prevented us from talking the entire way up, only adding to the suspense. Then, there at the top, sat our treasure pot, number twenty-five: our newest temporary home. The keys hung unsheltered on a hook by the door, just begging for someone, anyone, to snatch them away. I suppose this did at least explain the very cheap price for such "luxury".

It's funny to look back on these "disasters" but at the time it felt like one huge trick, like someone was watching us through hidden cameras as we clumsily tried to travel. We constantly questioned why it was so hard, no one else ever seemed to talk about things that went wrong but yet that was all that seemed to happen to us. Maybe other people were filtering, only showing the highs or maybe we were just problem prone.

Cautiously, we entered the apartment, hesitant as to what would be inside. However, behind the semi-soundproof door, it did offer the luxury we so longed for. Comfy sofas, clean surfaces and a restful feeling, that is, when the clanging and rumbling and drilling lessened. Completely contradicting the world outside the windows, the apartment was full of colour, vibrant clashing wallpapers, luminous kitchenware partnered with patterns and prints galore. How was this still perfectly intact when it was surrounded by such carnage? I couldn't find an answer so instead jumped face first onto the bed to try and find my own calm within the chaos.

Spirits partially re-lifted by the cosy room, we dumped our stuff and headed to buy supplies for the next few days, both agreeing, *(and promising,)* to only buy the basics.

Through no real choice of our own we had barely spent anything in Germany, it's hard to spend when there are no shops or you forget your wallets, so we were keen to keep this budget lifestyle going. We decided to look for instant noodles and microwave meals to help us stay on target, plus we would, of course, need eggs and bacon for breakfast.

Just like the courtyard beneath our room, our plan was shattered perilously. As we entered the supermarket, we were greeted by an olive counter the length of two double beds, at least. Ev has this vision every time we go away, that the true pinnacle of a holiday is the two of us relaxing on a balcony with wine and olives, like we're some aristocrats reminiscing on our beneficial property development rather than skint backpackers, and insists on purchasing so many olives each time we go anywhere, so obviously he was gone. And so was the list of "basics".

A quick plan change resulted in steaks for dinner that night and an unnecessary over-ingredient-ed spag-bol the next. And of course a vast selection of olives, and wines.

An overfilled trolley later, we heaved our stuff back into the building site, this time pleasantly greeted by no people and not a sound. The unnatural silence was unquestionably better than the constant drilling, smashing, and yelling from before. The darkness, however, was unsettling and with no way of knowing how to illuminate the wreckage, we walked briskly back up to our apartment.

Before preparing the steaks, of which we had decided to get two each as we were so very hungry, we unpacked our ridiculous amount of food. So much food that it overfilled the fridge. Then emptied the contents of our backpacks into the washing machine with half a bottle of Austrian non-bio and treated ourselves to our first hot showers in days.

Clean at last, and in relaxing comfort, we drank the wine and Ev grilled the steaks, like we'd done a thousand times at home. The food was delicious, double perfectly cooked steaks partnered with wine that wasn't thick or luminous. The familiarity of the evening was the comfort I'd been looking forward to; I felt truly content.

Maybe the backpacking life isn't so easy to adjust to, or maybe we weren't as low maintenance as we had hoped, or maybe we just needed some comfort after our time in that damp trailer. Either way the indulgence allowed an utter calmness to sweep over us. At least some good came out of our excessive shopping trip, as our credit balance dropped significantly.

Cosily settled into the lavishly decorated apartment, we talked about how best to spend the following day, settling on a plan to head out of this colourless world and back into the heart of Vienna to roam freely. Happy and relaxed, we spent the duration of the evening sprawled across the huge yellow sofa. I read aloud my latest editions to my book, then we played cards until we had finished the wine and were utterly exhausted.

A bed has never called me more. You would have thought we had been sleeping in a ditch for a month prior to arriving here, from the way we reacted to simple comforts. Compared to the hot and squashed single bed of the previous night, this bed felt like a slice of cloudy heaven. Without the fear of crawlies or an angry German ruler I fell into a deep slumber just moments after my head hit the pillow.

Chicken Crates

We slept gloriously, but alas, we were abruptly awoken when the builders returned. The entire apartment began to grumble as their deafening drills sank into the nearby walls. Barely able to comprehend our thoughts, let alone sleep any further, we dragged ourselves out of bed and set about gorging on a much needed breakfast feast.

Eggs, bacon, toast, beans and sausages cooked and piled in, we once again lay strewn across the sofa, uncomfortably bloated, trying desperately to ignore the clamour.

It was no use, the constant tool change and abundance of rumbling voices meant the sounds never plateaued enough to blend to the background. Constant surges of new noises, clangs, clacks, hums, crashes and thuds filled the apartment as the builders competed for the sound prize.

Reluctantly we decided to leave. A day lazing about on the sofa was what I really wanted. I had never walked as much as I had on this trip and so longed to be lazy and just take a restful pause, but the tenacious screeches and cranks of the bulldozer ensured that was never going to happen.

Before we left, we loaded the dishwasher haphazardly with salts and bubbles galore and packed in all of our dirtied crockery. An apparent error with unforeseen consequences that would greet us on our return that evening.

At last, we raced through the depressing detritus, away from the skull-cracking demolition, and in search of somewhere more welcoming. As we reached the station the silence was so thick it clouded over my ears, the lack of sound-intrusion wasn't as peaceful as I had hoped. My now empty ears felt fuzzy as they amplified any hints of noise detected. My tired brain almost willing me to go back before a constant ringing occupied my thoughts.

Yet again we struggled to navigate the trains, but after some begrudged support we made it into the city centre and began leisurely strolling around in the sizzling heat. Our sleepy heads, and legs, tired quickly of wandering within the overbearing crowds, so we headed off the main strip in search of some social solace.

Soon we found a well-hidden restaurant, tucked neatly down a side alley, and sat in the sun for a win, or two.

After we had topped up our alcohol levels and added more carbs to our bottomless bellies, we set off strolling again. Blearily blurred, the city felt calmer. We meandered up and down, through shops and bars, until finally we entered a luscious green park.

Instantly, we were accosted by two very drunk teenagers who were using the park's water pumps to dye their hair purple.
They cheered and screamed as they added more thick coatings of luminous dye. Their enjoyment was contagious; we laughed with them for a short while as they layered more and more violet paste through their locks. However, soon they offered to colour our hair, and as fun as it looked, we declined the offer and thought it best to move on quickly before we crumbled. Saying no to temptation is not something either of us had mastered, especially after a few midday wines.

Wandering with no real aim, we stumbled across a paragon; the most alluring patch of grass, shady but warm, populated but not swarmed, and most inviting of all was that most people upon it appeared to be napping.

Wordlessly we joined the slumber party and dozed in the sunshine, hoping no one would nick our loosely covered belongings.

After who knows how long we awoke; the park had darkened and almost emptied. We'd slept through the bustle of everyone waking up and moving on so we decided we too should leave. With apprehension we decided to venture back to the apartment, hoping that the builders would no longer be there. We strolled lazily through the park, and past remnants of hair dye on the newly stained cobbles.

I hoped that the new look wouldn't be too sobering for our temporary friends. As someone who has had countless, *countless,* hair dramas I know all too well how that first look in the mirror can shatter all delirious hopes that you once held. From bleach-blonde-orange to self-cut wonky fringe to gothic black, I've done it all and never once has it provided that *new-look-new-me* edge I'd hoped for.

As we stepped off the train, we noticed the same dull of vibrancy mirrored by warmth, in all meanings of the word, but to our delight the builders had finished for the day. Peace and quiet for a wine filled evening after a day napping in the sun, perfect. We could have skipped up the stairs with our quixotic hope for indulgence.

However, upon opening the door, we were welcomed by a bubbling stream gently shelling the apartment floor.

"What is that?" I froze, distantly hearing a low humming noise.

"For fuck's sake!" Ev exhaled as he paddled in. "It's the dishwasher," he called back.

It seemed the dishwasher had violently repelled all of its water, salts, foam and bubbles. Our luxurious apartment now looked like the aftermath of a soap bomb explosion at a bubble factory. Involuntarily, I too paddled my way through the spume to switch off the buzzing bubble blower.

Assessing the situation, we decided against telling the apartment owner, seeing as he had failed to tell us that we would be living within an active annihilation, this secret could be ours. Lazily, we swept the foaming river out of our apartment and into the empty hallway. No one else was here anyway, so who was to care?

******

As our inward journey had been so successful, and as I had somehow in my rigid itinerary forgotten to organise an outward journey, we decided to use the same means to leave Vienna and onto Budapest. Thankfully, we were able to book last minute seats for the following day.

So, the next morning, we trundled out of the construction site, much to the delight of the builders who upon seeing us loaded with our bags imminently set about destroying the last links from the ruins to our previous abode. We watched as they carelessly knocked it away, soapy bubbles still floating around the corridor.

Ev exhaled a deep laugh, "Where do you find these places?" He asked, but I sensed he didn't really need an answer. Plus I couldn't remember, I had entered an intense internet vortex whilst planning the trip and had no desire to dive back into it. We walked on ready for the next day of our adventure.

"Where are we meeting the driver?" Ev asked as he swigged his takeaway coffee.

"At the station." I replied, proud to have an answer ready.

"What side?" He chuffed his cigarette.

I paused, my communication with our soon arriving driver hadn't been of a great standard. "At the station." I repeated.

Ev laughed, "Did he say anything else?"

"He told us not to be late." All three of his brief messages had ended with, DO NOT BE LATE. An unusual and threatening email sign off.

As there was a small underpass connecting the opposing entrances, Ev stood at one end and directed me to wait at the other so we could call down if we saw the bottle green people carrier we were awaiting. After just a few minutes, we found ourselves childishly running backwards and forwards to each other rather than watching the road, which meant we were, in fact, late. Wonderful.

The interactions with the now jaded driver remained minimal. We smiled warmly; he did not. We tried to make small talk; he did not. I wished for the friendly chat of Pete and Michael. They had abolished my fears of murder instantly. In this case, the fears continued for the duration.

Evidently, the driver was a stern man, with a large car. A large car full of chicken crates. He instructed us to squeeze ourselves into the back and reassembled the (thankfully) empty chicken crates around us uncomfortably. This was about it for communication. Ev and I looked at each other from across the backseats, via corresponding gaps in crates, with a shared dread. This was not a situation I had ever imagined us to be in. My mind raced with questions, but I thought better than to interrogate the walking frown. Our presence had annoyed him enough.

I felt some comfort when another passenger jumped into the front seat. A girl who looked not much older than us with long red hair sauntered over and wordlessly sat in the front seat. I went to say hello but thought better of it when I saw her scowl at the driver. She was fierce and might bite if I made a sudden movement.

The two of them chatted the entire way in an aggressively heated manner, but never to either of us. I felt like we were invisible burdens, ignored but still causing annoyance by simply existing. People's unnecessary coldness is something that continues to baffle me. Ev and I are forgetful, unorganised, messy, careless but at least we smile at strangers and laugh at ourselves and at least try to be kind. Any hint of those normal interactions would have caused grave pain to our chaperones.

The journey took about three hours, but the discomfort internally and externally, made it feel so much longer. Time dragged its heavy heels whilst it laughed at my increasing anxiety. The argument continued throughout, raised voices, folded arms and sharp gesticulations kept it going and going and going.

Fortunately, we were freed on arrival (not anaesthetised and shoved into a chicken crate to be transported to our death as my racing brain had settled on when we turned down a dimly lit avenue).

Politely, we thanked him, to which he blatantly ignored and waited for us to get out of his car, way, and life forever.

Welcome to Retox

It was the hottest day yet, the sun blistered as we squeezed through Budapest's city crowds in search of our hostel. If only we never found it and instead unloaded our burdening bags in one of the many hammock-filled hostels we passed, or one of the gleaming hotels and then spent the afternoon enjoying our scenery. But no. We found it.

The desperate to be "cool" unnaturally-perfect-graffiti-decorated squirm-worthy, party hostel: Retox.

A place full of the cringiest examples of gap year non-conformist wannabes I have ever seen. On reflection we should have expected it, as this is the hostel's own sales line: ***This is not a place where people come to cleanse, rejuvenate or detox. It's a place where people come to drink, get wild, and RETOX.***

Utter cringe.

It was a skin crawling mix of organised fun, fake laughs, hedge funds, and insecurity-fuelled-judgement all squashed together in a prison style block of rooms surrounding an inner courtyard.

When I booked it, I had hoped it would be people up for a laugh and a night out, but mainly a chance for us to meet like-minded travellers. It was not. At all.

If you're reading this thinking that we went in there and judged everybody, and consequently thought we were cooler than cool, then I haven't yet made it clear just how awful it was.

Before we left home, we had expected to meet all sorts of people on this trip. People similar to us, people totally different to us - we were excited for it all. What we hadn't expected, or wanted, was to meet self-righteous, unworldly, sheltered, spoilt brats who pushed their idiotic ideologies on us.

It was very hard not to become too outwardly fed up, and completely winced. Especially when they looked at us like we were uneducated, as we didn't think this was the coolest place in the world.

Very quickly, the overwhelming cringeyness of Retox became too much, so we headed back out to buy some vodka, hoping that would make it more bearable.

Most of the countries we visited widely accepted the euro, but in those that didn't our rapid trips made it hard for us to grasp the exchange rates. So, when we were charged over ten thousand Hungarian forints for our vodka, we nearly passed out with shock.

The credit card was nervously produced and a high pitched "ding!" informed us of its success. I decided not to check the balance, our gluttony had caused us to spend double what we intended to in Vienna, and I didn't want to see what remained.

Later we found out that there was nothing to be concerned about, as it equated to around thirty euros, but for now we were cherishing the money draining vodka like a newborn baby. So on returning to Retox and being told by a girl who looked no older than sixteen that,

"If you put it down, I will drink iiiiiit, cos this is Retoooooooox." In a snarky go-with-the-flow fake voice, I didn't warm to the place any more than before.

To make things worse a *cooler-than-cool* mismatched-tattooed slimy-looking man approached me and said, "Just so you knooooow, if you're caught drinking your drink with your right hand someone will grab your aaaaaarse." He winked and waited for my response.

Instead, it was Ev who replied, "No you won't mate."

He said mate, but I highly doubt he'd intended anything friendly.

"Not yours maaaaan!" The lingering loser pushed on.

Ev stared at him and then very seriously sated, "If any one of you touch my girlfriend, I will knock you out." Never once has he even thrown a punch, let alone knock someone out but his words served their purpose and the man stepped back.

Rushing to his rescue a black-haired goth-princess shouted, "We don't maaaake the ruuuules." Then cackled whilst looking for support from her new peers.

I chugged some vodka, ensuring my left hand had a tight grasp on my cup.

They were all trying so hard to appear effortlessly rockstar, with put on whiny voices that dragged vowels so painfully. They repeatedly claimed to not care about *anything* but booze and getting drunk, but that just made it so apparent that this was not their natural habitat. Stop trying so hard and just have fun, my easy-breezy flower-power inner self was screaming.

We sat with the Retoxers for a while and watched them try to one up each other's stories of drinking, trying not to show our second-hand embarrassment. After what felt like years, a greasy long-haired guy who must have sold his soul to work there came into the room to make an announcement, "Hiiii guys. So tonight there's a pub crawl,-" Things were looking up "- it's us and a few other hostels all coming together. It's our chance to show that Retox really is the best hostel and we can out party all the others!" Everyone but us cheered the camp leader as he spoke.

He went on, "Make sure you're ready to drink and stay up all night, we're in this together." He was behaving as if it was some kind of cult movement heading into war, rather than a night out. "And no drugs guys. It's really strict here, don't let me down."

Hungary has some of the harshest drug laws in Europe, so much so that even possession of a minuscule amount of an illicit substance can result in two years imprisonment in an overcrowded jail.

The hardcore partiers all turned a translucent white at the mention of such atrocities, so we reasoned they were in no threat of being arrested.

Trying not to be noticed we contained our laughter at their repulsed shock, as it so perfectly followed their Jonny-Big-Bananas hard-line reveller acts, desperately avoiding eye-contact with one another. One glimpse and we would have Pseudobulbar-*ed*. I took me back to being at school, trying so hard not to laugh after being told off that you can't look even remotely towards your friend, or it would be game over. Ev and I often found ourselves in that situation, his booming voice always getting us caught. All these years later nothing's changed.

We went back to our room to get ready and quickly became acquainted with our roommates. Kindly, they informed us that if we hear people having sex not to worry as, *"This is Retooooooooox."* It was becoming more and more laughable how many times that phrase was used. Clearly the Retoxers idolised this place, we assumed it offered them a freedom that they hadn't experienced elsewhere, thus they felt it was the only place to find this kind of autonomy anywhere in the world.

As we progressed to the pub crawl, we hopefully expected to integrate into a chilled-out group of people to drink and have a laugh with. Instead, we were met with more sheltered sanctimonious weirdos who had been allowed a weekend without a watchful eye of their parents or of their middle-class society that they so clearly wanted to dominate but pretended to hate *"all that capitalist shit."*

It's so easy to disregard education and wealth when you've got it and are comfortably aware that it isn't going anywhere. When you're returning home from university without fees because your parents have paid for it up front, or a six-figure starting salary because of your connections (both examples were given, and then followed with *but I don't need that shiiiiiit*). Why pretend to be someone you're not? You've got an advantage, don't be a dick about it, own it or change it. Fake people are by far the most infuriating. You can't help what you're born into and shouldn't be ridiculed for that - at either end of the unbalanced class scale- but you most definitely can help the integrity in which you present yourself.

Thankfully within this draining crowd, consisting of over three hundred people, were just two other normal people for us to chat to. A Swedish couple completing a trip similar to ours, again there's seemed to have gone much smoother from what they shared, no angry German hosts, or demolished apartments or even any interactions with armed guards.

As the evening progressed into night, we were less able to conceal our humour when again and again we heard the phrases, *"This is Retooooooooox,"* or *"Welcome to Retoooooooooooooox,"* especially as we were now not even physically at Retox, but obviously they informed us that *"It's not just a plaaaaaace it's a way of liiiiiiifffe."* Our blatant amusement resulted in us being shunned as, *"You just don't get iiiiiiiiiiiiiiiiiiiit."* Which to be fair, was more than true.

After a few painful hours we broke away from the crowd to explore the night alone. Unsurprisingly we had a lot more fun drinking and dancing just the two of us. But as always when I have too much fun (or alcohol), I get the Deathly Hiccups that can only be cured by ingesting mouthful upon mouthful of sugar. After desperately explaining this to an unsuspecting kebab shop owner, Ev returned with a small pot of white sugar, my hero. I chomped it down as we walked indiscriminately around the darkened city.

Accidentally, we bumped into some Retoxers who, undeniably, thought the sugar was the aforementioned contraband. Their wide eyes ran off, gasping in fear that they would gain an associated charge, which only added to our entertainment.

After I consumed all the sugar, then violently threw up, we devoured some pizza from a street vendor before reluctantly strolling back to Retox. As a last effort to "get it," we drank in the hostels' bar for a few more hours, whilst the natives judged, and eye-rolled at us.

Earlier in the day, we had crammed all of our stuff onto the bottom bunk of our allotted beds. So, when we finally retired to sleep, we decided against moving it all and instead cosily shared our top bunk in this overcrowded dorm room.

After about an hour, we unmistakably heard the echoed sounds of a girl being sick in the shower, and, of course, in between retching, she croaked the phrase, "*Welcome to Retooooooox*," which set us off in cringed hysterics once again, this time we made no effort to conceal them.

Retox was supposed to be cool. It most definitely wasn't, but it was meant to be and was somewhere we had looked forward to, so even though I felt certain of the answer I felt nerves twirling in my stomach when I broached the question quietly to Ev, "Shall we get out of here tomorrow? Rather than stay another night? We could find a different hostel? Less people? A pool maybe?" Before my nervous babbling could proceed, he responded, "Definitely." and kissed my head. Our opinions were aligned and our social shunning, and tolerance of the stupid, couldn't take much more.

If I didn't know already, I knew then this was the person for me, he didn't pretend to like it here like everyone else must have been doing, and he didn't need a solid escape plan just the thought of something better. He was a lot more go with the flow than I was, that was enough of a plan for him and he slipped soundly to sleep. I however spent the next hour googling nearby hostels (without any luck) on my phone desperate for a tangible plan.

As soon as the uncomfortable pain of morning arrived, we gathered our things and burst into the street with no further plans. We'd rather swallow the financial loss than spend any longer in this sweaty dive. The morning brought not only hangovers but an unmovable smell of shame. The once partiers panicked over their drunken actions, we overheard many a phone call home and fretful conversions about their alcohol consumption. The beer fear was here, and we did not want to be.

Once again loaded up like camels in the desert we set about exploring Budapest's highlights in the blazing sun; it was another unbearably scoring day. Jumping from shade to shade we soon gave in and instead searched for a room for the night. Not dissimilar to Mary and Joseph we were told over and over that there was no room. Our quest continued. Longingly we entered, and consequently exited, hotels with outdoor pools that we most definitely couldn't afford. Each rejection made the next entry harder, as if it was a personal attack rather than a capacity issue. The sweaty pilgrimage took us further and further out of the city.

Finally, someone took pity on us, and offered us an empty room (thankfully with no inhabiting barn animals or the impending arrival of a baby).

The only bonus of yet another remote residence was that we were near the bus station; the following day we were catching a bus to Croatia's capital, Zagreb, so hopefully waking up nearby would reduce the chance of us being late, lost or lavish.

Our room was basic. Four walls that were once white but now held a dusky grey, no windows, and a metal framed double bed that almost touched each wall. Plus we had access to a communal toilet in the garden (!?). Without much need to, or any space to do so, we didn't unpack, just lay ourselves on the uncomfortable bed desperate to cool down.

We sun hid for as long as our hunger would let us and then re-emerged like haggard butterflies from a booze-cruise of a chrysalis. Following yet another considerable stroll of food hunting, we ended our second day in Budapest by celebrating the Chinese mid-autumn festival with about two hundred other people in a raucous Chinese restaurant.

Love and laughter surrounded us as we ate dish after dish of aromatic delights. Who knew we'd feel more ourselves at a Chinese festival than on a pub-crawl.

IDIOTIC SIDE OF THINGS

Yet again we woke up early to lug ourselves, and worldly belongings (inflatable sofa that we never inflated, an over enthusiastic Swiss army knife, fully stocked first aid kit) into the unknown. Today's journey started by fearfully crossing a busy motorway to another completely isolated bus station. Initially, we were the only people there and once again the internal panic began effervescing. Desperately, I scanned the barren surroundings for help. It really isn't meant to be this hard, is it?

Fortunately, it wasn't too long until other people joined us and I relaxed again. My constant rollercoaster of emotions had begun for the day. Soon enough the coach pulled in; we settled ourselves on board and happily waved goodbye to Budapest, and our Retoxing frenemies.

The journey was easy. A midway pitstop allowed us to snack, smoke and stroke a litter of stray puppies before being forcefully warned off by the protective mother.

Once again I browsed Ev's brain for more answers of the universe, (What if everyone in the world suddenly looked exactly the same, and couldn't speak, would you know who I was?
If I lost all my teeth and shaved my head would you still fancy me?
Would you rather never see daylight again, or always be in direct sunlight?)

On arriving in Zagreb, we found our hostel without a problem and promptly set out for the rest of the day. A towering building caught our eye. More specifically, the bar sitting seductively at the top of it.

We decided to enter and take in the city from above. A short lift ride to the top floor took us to the lavish, and mostly empty, wine bar. The perfect setting for insolvent backpackers? Not quite, but we decided a few glasses couldn't hurt and that may have been true if we hadn't engaged in a lengthy conversation with one of the hovering bartenders about his family's vineyard and were then unable to decline his eagerness for us to try bottle after bottle of his "family wine."

Another day's budget blown. Our credit card limit of forty euros per day had been exceeded every single day since we'd set it. In actual fact we had nearly spent another eight hundred euros. Thankfully, we only had two more stops after this, so there was absolutely no chance we'd spend it all. Right?

After a hefty wine tasting, at a deceptively discounted price, we moved to the balcony, to relieve our dizzy brains with fresh air and to escape the eager salesman. As we admired the bustling world below, it didn't take us long to spot a hubbub of people weaving in and out of a village of white tents.

Eager to explore we avoided eye-contact from the predator behind the bar and made for the lift. Tipsily tainted, we stumbled out of the serenity and, by chance, right into Zagreb's food and film festival full of life and noise.

Everyone was smiling; the park was alive with a buzzing energy; sizzling aromas filled our noses and led us to local delicacies. Instantly immersed, we guzzled beers and once again filled our stomachs until we were merrily walking back towards the hostel in dusky hues. It seemed at last the drama was passing, temporarily anyway.

Somehow the wine bar seemed even more alluring in the dark, bright lights circulated the summit and drew us up as if we were weightless. We swore to one another that we would just have *one* more drink, which obviously didn't happen.

We sampled more local wines and played Ludo on a large wooden board until the early hours of the morning. Ev had never come across this mind-numbing children's board game before plus our obsessive card playing was wearing thin on us both, consequently the new entertainment and never ending wine glasses were hard to leave.

As the hours ticked on, and the city below emptied, the staff were began tidying around us. The bar drew nearer to its closing time. By this point even the wine-raptor had had enough of our childish giggles. Finally, we were asked to leave.

Completely drunk, we just about stumbled back to our hostel to try and catch some sleep before our early flight to Split, now just hours away. Unsurprisingly, the following morning didn't go as planned.

Yet again I had set our early morning alarms for the afternoon (!!) and consequently, we overslept. Seriously, what is wrong with me? Ev was not pleased, to say the least. On reflection, I don't know why I continued to be responsible for the alarms, as I am clearly incapable of focusing on the task at hand.

Frantically, we scrambled about the room trying, and failing, not to wake the other traveller in our dorm. We ran to the bus stop and realised that we had, of course, missed our intended airport shuttle, and the next one wouldn't arrive for an hour and therefore wouldn't get us to the airport in time. Great.

Feeling guilty, and painfully hungover, I offered to haul a cab. I was unsuccessful, due to an overwhelming lack of passing traffic. The streets were always empty when we were in crisis which just added an (unwanted) eerie spice to the fear.

Time was soaring again, and we were not moving any nearer to the airport just frantically pacing up and down the road. After a few minutes of no change occurring, we decided to just walk (run) towards the airport with the hope of finding a cab on the way.

With no real clue where to go we tried to follow the road signs, as we moved way too fast for people who had been drinking wine all night. Each new road we turned down held no cabs, just more land for my achy feet to cover. The further we ran, the more I doubted our arrival. Until suddenly we were out of town and at the edge of the motorway, sat above it was a road sign with the words "zračna luka" and a picture of a plane. We had no choice but to join the sea of speeding traffic, on foot.

So off we went, sprinting along the motorway, dragging our stuff (dressing gown, oversized sun hat, sixteen pairs of sunglasses) carelessly behind us, just a few groggy hours after our spinning heads had hit the pillows.

Cars honked aggressively and drivers shouted passing insults but there were still no cabs. All the wine from the previous night sloshed around in my stomach sickeningly, but I dared not stop. A car would hit me, or the hangover-reaper would, at last, take me in his grips. Plus, our funds were so low (somehow we'd already spent one-thousand euros on the credit card?!) that I feared if we missed any of our prepaid connections, we would be stuck where we stood, *forever*. We definitely didn't have enough for new flights to Split, let alone a new route home.

Early morning marathon completed; we finally saw the airport. Just as we slowed to catch our breath, a cab conveniently pulled up. We piled in, hot and breathless. It seemed people were always there to help right at the last minute, but anything would have been better than continuing the death run we'd endured. We arrived just in time, sweaty, exhausted and grouchy, but on time and not stranded. Success!

A short plane ride later we touched down in Split, then boarded a bus that was supposed to take us right to our hostel on the coast. Or "near enough", as we were assured after being kicked out at the bottom of a winding hill. This time it was flashbacks of Genoa that caused the panic, the thought of having to scale another uninviting colossus was hair-raising. It seemed I was going to go home traumatised by my own dramatic narratives and consequently have a multitude of new unnecessary anxieties when, in fact, I should have been having fun.

Thankfully, Ev is much more of a *cool-headed-cucumber* and noted a less steep route up.

After a not too strenuous ascent, and this time with absolutely no cheese sauce flowing from my face orifices, we checked into Ladybird Hostel: my favourite lodging of the entire trip. Completely unexpected, so fun, chilled, and just what we needed after the letdown at Retox, and the fly-by trip to Zagreb.

We dropped our stuff into our room and made our way to the small but welcoming common area. The walls were covered in colourful signatures from guests gone by, names, pictures, and memories all painted onto the shared space.

Immediately, we were greeted by two enthusiastic Norwegian lads, both sporting a sun kissed glow that didn't suit their fair complexions, as if someone had layered them in too much fake tan. One of them looked weathered by his travels; he had a poorly shaved head paired with a stubbly chin. On top of his head sat a blue pair of those unflattering wrap around sunglasses men so often opt for, making him look like a prickly cyborg.

The other one had longer unkempt, blonde-highlighted hair and piercing green eyes. He was wearing a thin light blue t-shirt with the words "SPLIT BOAT PARTY" printed across the front.

Sitting slightly behind them with a humoured yet bemused look on his face was an English traveller who we would get to know a bit better over the next few days, but more presently, why he was withholding such expression.

The Norwegian guys, (who never revealed their real names, just referred to themselves as "You Wish You Were Here." No matter how much grammatical explanation we gave they insisted that was them) offered us some beers and we joined them to play cards.

The beers, and then vodka, sank quickly and soon our chats became serious. We descended into that intense kind of sternness that only comes from intoxication. When you feel you understand the world around you better than anyone else and are so keen to share your point and to be heard- *over and over again.* Their all-knowing-ness came when they divulged that they had met one another at a seminar, back home in Oslo, dedicated to the art of "Pulling women."

"It's a select group of people with a shared aim." The prickly one was carefully selecting his words. "We discuss our theories and experiences."

"It's groundbreaking psychological science," Green Eyes added.

I caught the eye of the guy behind, Jasper, and he raised his eyebrows in a way that said, *idiots, right?*

I stifled a laugh but returned the sentiment thus inviting him to join our table. He shuffled over, pleased he wasn't alone in his disbelief.

"Tell them what you told me about the dessert." Jasper probed them, whilst grinning devilishly at us. Attaining allies was clearly fuelling his confidence to question them.

It's crazy how much communication can be made silently between people when there's a shared commonality, in this case the intrigue/disbelief/ridicule of these strange over-confident men.

"No, we don't need to share." The prickly one stiffened up.

"Come on! Don't hide crucial information." Ev teased for the benefit of Jasper, and thankfully his tone sailed way over You Wish You Were Here's heads.

"I dont think it's necessary." Green Eyes was more wavering in his tone.

"I could help, maybe?" I offered.

"Help? Why do we need your help?" Prickly prickled.

"I just thought if you're taking these classes about women, and there's multiple theories maybe I could offer some inside information. Test the theories, tell you my side. You know, as a woman."

Jasper kicked my leg supportively under the table, he was keen for other people to hear what he had heard.

The Norwegians looked at each other, Green Eyes nodded.

"Okay. The Dessert Theory. "Prickles sat up and made sure everyone was looking at him, we were in for a treat - I could feel it.

"When out for a meal with a woman, her choice in dessert will tell you a lot. Presently it will divulge her sexual interest, and then on a deeper level her overall intentions." He paused for reaction.

"Go on." Ev pushed.

Prickles looked at him, he was debating what to say.

"Tell them about Hedda." Green Eyes pushed his shoulder gently.

"Hedda, ahh." Prickles looked down; this was going to take a while. "I dated Hedda for six months. I liked her a lot, I loved her in fact. But then." He paused again.

"Then?" I was invested.

"Strawberries." Green Eyes stated.

We stared back wordlessly.

Prickles continued, "I took Hedda out to a nice restaurant in Oslo. Very expensive, very good meal. We had many wines and chatted happily. It was a wonderful night, but then." he paused again.

"Strawberries?" I offered.

Causing Ev and Jasper to let out poorly contained laughs. In sync they picked up their drinks and tried to hide smirks.

"But then," he continued, ignoring us all, "it was time for dessert. We looked at the menu. There were many things, nice things. You know what she picked?"

"Strawberries?" Ev laughed.

"She ordered strawberries and vanilla ice cream." he exhaled dramatically, he had just reached the summit of his story and was wanting a dramatic reaction.

"So terrible." Green Eyes consoled him.

"Just the worst." Jasper joined in.

"Please explain." I was not sharing their emotion and was desperate to understand.

"As I said, a woman's choice in dessert will tell you a lot. Presently it will divulge her sexual interest, and then on a deeper level her overall intentions." He repeated his starting statement with robotic precision.

"So, what did the strawberries tell you?" I pushed.

Prickles and Green Eyes shared a soundless look, one between friends who shared a sadness, a grief.

Green Eyes sighed.

"Strawberries," Prickles shook his head, "Strawberries tell us she is a liar. She had nothing naughty left."

I cringed at the use of "naughty" and tried desperately not to look at Ev or we would have erupted.

"Before, the sex had been very good, the strawberries showed me that was over. She was a liar. She had said she loved me, she didn't. It was all lies."

I could hear his words, understand them, yet still nothing made sense. I stared at him, and he continued.

"So, after she ordered I wished her goodnight and I left. We've never seen each other again."

"What?! You just left? The woman you loved, you just left." I exclaimed.

"Yes, it was clear to me that she had lied."

"Did you ask her that? Or you just assumed?" I couldn't believe what I was hearing.

"Not assume. It was the dessert."

Ev spurted his drink, and then covered it with, "Course, strawberries." Shooting me a wink.

I had so many questions and was so enraged by this idiocy, "Did you ever explain to her what happened? A phone call at least."

"No."

"That poor woman, you just left her there over some strawberries."

"You don't understand, she was a liar."

Why is it that the most stupid are always the most confident in their thoughts? So unwavering and closed minded when their words are just jelly. No substance, no seriousness, just absolute wobble.

Sensing my rage, Ev acted to move us away from the heartbroken woman sat alone and confused, and rewrite the end of the story, "What if she had ordered something else then. Like, cheesecake?"

Green Eyes sat up, "Ah cheesecake. If only."

"Cheesecake is honest, true, pure. Cheesecake is a lot of sex." Prickles puffed his chest out.

My face fell into my hands.

The conversation moved on, naturally, and soon they felt I was a fount of wisdom. Ideas based on people as individual,s who will tell you how they feel rather than require you to search for hidden clues and deeper meanings seemed farfetched and baffling to them. After a while You Wish You Were Here asked to record me as I spoke in conversation. I politely refused.

They "slyly" filmed me anyway. I wonder if I'll be used as a subject to analyse in their next seminar. A room full of predatory men awestruck by the thought of a woman sharing intentions rather than discreetly hinting at them.

Thankfully, the common room filled up and by early evening we had quite a crowd of us, You Wish You Were Here left and the more normal of us drank together. Our new crowd was made up of me, Ev, corner-Jasper, a happy-go-lucky and stunningly beautiful Swedish woman called Anna, Olivia a stocky German woman with a thick brown bob that had been cut so bluntly it looked like a comedy wig, and a couple of vibrant Spanish nurses (Salma and Sofia). We played games and chatted freely for hours. You Wish You Were Here made a brief appearance, much to the dismay of Anna, as it turned out they had all been on a party boat for the last ten days, and the uncomfortable confinement with their women-wisdom had become unbearable for her.

Happily, drunk, our gang headed into town. We soon came across a beach club. Cheesy DJs and open-air dancing was exactly what this night needed, so we swifty entered and danced euphorically on the sand. As our feet tired, we retired to the more loungey side of the bar, slumping down on beanbags to drink cocktails.

Somehow, we had unintentionally stumbled into the filming of what I can only assume is the Croatian equivalent to, *Made in Chelsea*. This fake-reality seriousness was too tempting for Ev, who was adamant to be in the background doing something stupid. Strolling past and breaking the third wall by glancing right at the camera or creating dramatic gesticulations in response to their *very important* conversations, and then finally he nestled himself within the "cast" and began gossiping idly.

Initially, the cast members didn't realise he was an intruder so temporarily he had a chance to make the final cut, but his overpowering voice and extravagant reactions alerted the directors who angrily ushered him away. By this point we were all bent over laughing, but the fury on the "celebrities" faces confirmed that we were alone in the amusement. Taking that as our cue to leave we exited the club and continued into the night.

Giggling girlishly, we wandered about the beautiful city. We ambled through narrow alleys in the maze of streets that make up the old town. In turn each one opened up to cobblestoned courtyards where bars and pubs shared the bedazzled outdoor space. The combination of this historical setting combined with the energetic buzz of the evening made it feel like we had entered a noughties rom-com. All we needed was Adam Sandler to appear in an oversized shirt arm-in-arm with a bohemian beauty and we'd be there.

We sat in an illuminated courtyard, drank beers, and swapped stories of home and travelling, bucket lists and obstacles. Each one of us so different to the next but sharing that peacefulness which can only be truly reached whilst away from life's daily stresses.

Soon enough we were ready to leave, but the overworked staff had other ideas.

"This is taking forever." Anna moaned as she effortlessly swished her white hair over her shoulder, stunning about six men in her vicinity.

Looking around playfully Ev suggested, "Shall we just go."

Jasper's dark eyes lit up.

"What and not pay?" Sofia looked interested, her dark purple lips lifted at the corners.

"No way! Not at all." Salma refused to even acknowledge the idea.

Anna and I were keen, silently we'd shared a nod of I-know-we-shouldn't-but-I-definitely-want to.

Another ten minutes of waiting passed.

"Come on, we're going." Ev told the group.

"There's no other option." Olivia had been quiet on the topic until now, stern in words and in stature.

"No." Salma crossed her arms.

Sofia spoke to her quickly in Spanish, I assume something like "Stop spoiling the fun, we want to leave here you're being difficult."

"No."

"Maybe we'll just go then." I teased.

She rolled her eyes.

"After three we all stand up then head over there," pushing on with his plan Ev pointed to a dimly lit passageway.

Jasper looked around for any staff members.

"Are you serious? What if we get caught?" Salma flapped.

"Then we just say that we've asked for the bill, and we need to leave right now and then maybe they'll finally let us pay, what's the worst that can happen?" Jasper reasoned.

"Okay, fine." She didn't look fine, but her words were enough to confirm her participation.

Plan agreed, we all stood at once- maybe a little too synchronised- looked sheepishly at one another and then clumsily pushed our way through the rabble. Instantly our seats were filled by another group in this buzzy void.

Alive with fear, we tore through the passageways with the urgency as if we had robbed a bank and then flew out into another, quieter, courtyard. Laughing wildly at our success.

"Guys, stop." Salma puffed.

"What's wrong?" I asked.

"I left my jacket there! I need to go back!"

Returning to the scene of the crime is exactly what you shouldn't do if you intend to get away, yet criminals always seem to find their way back.

She insisted we all return with her, as this had been our "Stupid idea" in the first place. So, we all, supportively yet slyly, snuck back through the alleys. In a pink panther-esq style she darted in and retrieved it without a hiccup. We were free- again!

The night continued as we bar crawled through the city. After a while we were down to just five of us, four of which were desperate for a night swim in the sea. Majority-vote ruled, so we stumbled out of the old town and down to the coast. The stoney beach was nestled perfectly beside the harbour. Standing on the edge of the peninsula looking over the sea with almost no light around was totally breath-taking. The seemingly endless ocean reflected the moon's glare as it dared us to enter.

The four of us who were ignoring all sensible suggestions to not enter the freezing choppy water whilst our body content had likely reached eighty-percent alcohol ran frivolously into the waves. The sensible one guarded the clothes and laughed at our idiocy. We frolicked and splashed and shivered. Immediately my freckled skin was covered in cold-induced goosebumps. Ev and I played adoringly, sea-lovers by day and night. Laying in the forceful waves admiring the stars whilst hand in hand with the love of my life is a memory I'm keen to hold forever.

"I love you, Goose." He kissed my frozen nose.

"I love you too," I beamed through chattering teeth.

"I've had such a good time." He looked around our new surroundings, and towards our temporary friends.

"Really?" My heart was full.

"Yeah, its been great." He paused, "But maybe we'll plan it together next time." With that he playfully splashed a tidal wave in my direction then ducked under the water to avoid any retaliation.

Finally, the cold fully took over and we could no longer bear it. It was time to get out and dash back to the hostel for warmth. Only now we noticed that Salma and Jasper were entangled at the mouth, and it took us a lot of splashing and jeering to get them to disengage.

After a wet walk home Ev and I laid down that night feeling happy and free and chatted endlessly about all the adventures we'd had and will continue to have, knowing it will always be us that's on the idiotic side of things. But if that meant more ridiculousness and happy thoughts then that's fine by me.

COMPLETELY CLUELESS

Clouded by a sleep-induced booze-fog, we dragged ourselves to the common room, where we found our new friends looking and feeling much the same. Mutually, we decided a big breakfast would sort us out and as a swarm moved towards the beach for a fry up.

The way fried food and carbs lure the sickly hungover only to double back and increase their self-sabotaging feeling is a vicious game, but not one we're quick to learn from. Fruit, a shower and some fresh air? No thank you, I'll take excessive calories brutishly greased together whilst I try to remain still enough not to vomit.

Over a shamefully large breakfast, Salma and Sofia revealed they had rented a car for the day and offered us, and Jasper, a lift to a nearby quieter beach. Excitedly, we all agreed.

A day that was destined for a hungover mope had just been massively improved. Thankfully the sky was overcast giving our pounding heads a break from the harsh blaring sun. We could just about manage laying very still by gentle water, hopefully away from the crowds. With the food in our bellies swirling with the remaining booze and consequently enhancing the nausea, we ambled back towards the hostel in hope the beach would help.

Quickly we loaded up the car and set off. As I'd had no control whatsoever, (planning, navigating or even fully aware of where we were heading,) we arrived without a glitch.

The secluded beach was vast and almost empty. Smooth grey stones rattled beneath us as we trudged across them; the water washing them gently whilst nipping at our toes. We tried our best to make comfort on this inflexible surface, but all lay strewn awkwardly. I closed my eyes and listened to the calm water, feeling full appreciation of today's break from panic, stress and movement. We must have spent hours lolling about, calmly lazing in the water and chatting futilely. Then the rain came.

Like always, just an initial drop here and there that we chose to ignore, then, within seconds, the entire sky let loose, and the torrent began. Huge droplets splash landed all around us as we darted back to the car, our hangovers requisitely jet washed off us. Soaked through, we sat in the car and hoped it would pass. It didn't. The rain got heavier and distantly we saw faint flashes, followed by thundering booms. Evidently, it was time to leave. I was so pleased not to be driving. Vision heavily impaired, winding roads, and impatient locals made the journey back a quiet yet intense one. Our tyres skidded through deceptively deep puddles, cars honked, and drivers screamed as we slowed on each blind bend all the while the windscreen became more and more blurred.

Inside the car was silence, as we bounced into one another swerving this way and that way. I wondered if I'd die here in this rainy Croatian town, crashed into by an impatient driver or swept into the sea by another forceful puddle wave.

Our return journey took almost four times as long as our outward one. As soon as the engine was switched off, we let out a communal sigh of relief followed by thankful laughter. It was time for a celebratory drink. We all cheered Salma for returning us home injury free and promptly poured her a vodka.

The rain continued late into the orange-hued evening and our accommodating host let us drink in the common room until much later than, "Usual curfew". With each lightning flash, the room was illuminated through the make-shift sheet roof, and sparse glacial drips rolled down our unsuspecting backs.

As I refilled with booze, my confidence, (or stupidity,) returned, "Swim?" I suggested to the group.

"Yes!" Salma was the first to agree tonight.

"Nah not tonight," Jasper responded.

I looked to Ev, he smiled with twinkling eyes, "No, you two go."

My eyes must have quadrupled, I couldn't go without him. He's my safety blanket and here I am doing stupid things. He needs to be there too.

As if understanding all my racing thoughts Ev caught my eye and nodded, encouraging me to go without him. This was not the plan.

"Okay, just us." I smiled at Salma, looking calm but definitely not feeling it. Like how a duck floats so majestically on the surface yet below its legs and paddling like mad. That was me, I was the duck. Or rather, the Goose, now without her Ev.

I waited for him to change his mind, silently pleading it. He didn't. Just minutes later we left the others and made a dash towards the sea through the relentless storm. As we ran in the rain, my separation anxiety eased and I laughed and howled with my new friend.

We found a small hut on the beach to stash our clothes, and before the coldness could sway our bleary minds, we dived headfirst into the tumbling waves. Letting the rain pelt our pimpled skin, we bobbed about, drinking cheap wine from the bottle and screaming with happiness.

We shared secrets and chatted girlishly about our plans for the future. It seemed her interaction with Jasper last night had caught her interest. She asked about what I thought life would be like for me and Ev as we got older, and I dreamed aloud of babies and pets and travels galore.

When our skin resembled that of eighty year old raisins and our lips were a quivering blue we finally rolled our way out of the water. We made a sharp dash for our shielding hut, the only light reflecting from the bright white cloudless moon above. Instantly, the cold air covered my skin like an icy blanket, and my body began to convulse. My numb fingers fumbled for my clothes. Then, total fear froze me completely.

Within moments of our return, terrifying looming shadows snuck under the hut's walls; it was evident that we had been surrounded. We looked at each other with wide, panicked eyes. Before we had time to think, an unfamiliar face peeked in. His eyes lit up excitedly like that of a person who has had an unexpected lottery win. He spoke eagerly to the other shadows. More unfamiliar male faces filled the only exit point of our hut. I was completely terrified, cold, wet, basically naked, drunk and now trapped. The slimy looking men talked frantically to one another. One even lent in and grabbed my arm viciously, to which my reactive flinch made them cackle menacingly. They crowded brutishly to watch as we stood there defenceless, imagining the worst.

I had never wished for Ev to appear like a knight in shining armour more. I knew I shouldn't have gone out without him. Every second that passed I reduced in size, soon I'd be just a foot tall cowering beneath these predators.

Faced with the challenge, Selma reacted in the complete opposite to my shrinking-self and inflated with courage. She spoke assertively to them in an unknown (to me) language.

Mid speech she gestured towards me. Temporarily, I thought she had sacrificed me to save herself, but then she stood in the way like my personal bodyguard, scowling with unwavering confidence. I was in utter awe of her. The men, however, seemed enraged at whatever she had said and thus my fear increased. They jeered nastily and sneered at each other. I saw them as a clan, rather than individuals, six, maybe seven, tall thin men with black eyes and long noses. The more I looked the longer their limbs seemed, fingers like drumsticks on the end of ten-foot arms all threatening to engulf me and disappear into the night.

Covertly Salma whispered, "Just play along," which was completely pointless as I had no idea what was happening. She conversed further and argued well, or so it appeared that way, and finally they backed away ever so slightly. I was still completely clueless as to all that had occurred, but with their movement, we grabbed our clothes and forced our way out. Salma led me by the hand, and they jeered at us as we ran fearfully in the darkness.

When we were certain we weren't being followed, we doubled over breathlessly, buzzing with relief.

Salma panted, "I didn't even know I could speak Italian so well!"

So had not only saved the day but had impressed herself, and me, greatly! In relieved shock to have escaped we laughed about our fearsome experience and linked arms for our now more casual retreat.

"What just happened?" I laughed in confusion.

"Well first of all I asked them what they wanted."

"It was clear what they wanted." I replied.

"Yes, but I needed to hear them talk so I knew what language." She said this as if it's a skill we all possess, instead of it being some kind of superpower.

"Then I told them we were in a relationship, and no one should dare mess with my heiress English girlfriend or jeopardise our new relationship!"

Her fierce protection had worked, whether they believed her lie or not.

"Heiress?!" I exclaimed.

"I got carried away." She squealed, squeezing my arm tighter.

This, I had no problems with and was grateful for her protection. What I did have a problem with was her now uncomfortably changing the mood.

"You know I've kissed girls before." I could feel her eyes burning my cheek. "It's much more fun than guys."

I felt my enjoy body stiffen up as she flicked her hair and moved her hand slowly down from my elbow towards my hand.

"You can thank me for saving you when we get back," she winked and giggled wildly.

She was actually suggesting that I should thank her for saving me from the leachy men by behaving like a leachy woman.

As a person who is awkward in most should-be-comfortable situations, I reacted with the friendliness of a pirate's walking plank.

Thankfully, we arrived back at the hostel before anything was forced any further.

However, this hostel had an odd, and impractical, shower set up, in that the only two were in one uncomfortably small room and merely separated by a translucent curtain.

Initially we entered a shower each, but after constantly readjusting the curtain and rejecting Salma's *many* advances, I fled mid-lather and nestled into bed with a peacefully snoring Ev.

I hugged a little tighter that night and hoped no one else would try to get me. He rolled over and took me into his arms, "Well done." He whispered, pleased I had left his side in an unknown place and not let my anxiety run wild.

I decided to tell him about the creepy men and creepy Salma in the morning, for now he could think I was able to survive without him.

I closed my eyes as my bubble covered body hiccupped me to sleep.

Everyone First Class

The rain pushed on throughout the night and lazily through to the following morning. I was pleased that for once we didn't have to wake up and instantly rush off to the next place; we weren't leaving until that evening when we would catch an overnight ferry back to Italy. We shielded from the rain and added our mark to the vibrant visitor-signed walls. I painted a huge sunflower across our bedroom wall and signed our names in swirly colourful letters, and then beamed like a toddler who'd come home from nursery with an incomprehensible piece of artwork as Ev praised my efforts.

We planned to spend the duration of the day capering cobbled lanes and leisurely packing up for the penultimate time, now so close to the end of this turbulent feat. One final destination, Senigallia, for a few days lazing on the beach before finally heading home.

Whilst wandering, the light pattering rain evolved into enormous bubbles bursting all around us, disrupting our peaceful amble. We dashed for shelter under a flapping yellow canopy protruding from a nearby doorway to watch the water tumble down. Something twinkled on the other side of the door and caught our wandering eyes, so we peered in nosily.

The room itself was poorly lit, but within it we could see rows of wooden cabinets illuminated with their own individual spotlights. Only now we realised it was some sort of exhibition and lubberly pushed our way in to find out more. It unfolded that we had unintentionally stumbled across the infamous stuffed frog museum. The most curious place I have ever visited.

We immediately purchased tickets and began perusing the hundreds and hundreds of taxidermied frogs. Frog Olympics, frog classrooms, rowing frogs, circus frogs and they'd even posed some half-frogs as if they were submerged in water. Whatever you can imagine, they had it, in frog form. An absolute treasure trove of peculiar entities, both in and out of the boxes. To work and purposely visit "Froggyland" there is surely a bit of strange about you, us included. What a way to end our visit to Croatia.

All frogged out, we returned for the last farewell to Ladybird Hostel then made our way to catch the ferry. The port had an empty silence about it. A skeleton staff, and hardly another customer in sight. Their vague and unconvincing directional waves didn't fill us with confidence as we waited to board one of the stationary boats. Our ticketed time of departure came and went and still, no one knew where we should wait, or which ferry would be ours. Blank faces and shrugged shoulders met each of our questions.

Maybe we were used to this disruption by now, or maybe it was because it was late in the day, but we didn't panic in that now over-familiar, frantic energy. Instead, we just plateaued helplessly. We slumped down on the dock to continue yet another game of cards, surprisingly unbothered by the lack of information. Maybe I was learning to relax a little after all. Or, more likely, I had given up all hope of easy travel.

Suddenly, one of the unhelpful staff members ran at us, flailing his arms and calling for us to follow him. In a flurry, he raced us across to another dock and hollered out to the staff, who were already wrenching up the bridge, to wait for us. Their sharp gesticulations and stern look suggested that this was not the first time he had failed to shepherd all customers to the correct dock in a timely fashion. Feeling like maybe we should have panicked, or pursued a little more, we apologised awkwardly. Wobbling up a half-secured bridge, I was eager to ensure that we were directed to the right place once on board; I had opted to upgrade us to First Class and wanted to make sure that those two extra euros (!!) were not ignored. Immediately I informed a member of staff that our seat was upgraded to which she replied, "Yes, yes everyone First Class. Follow crowd please."

Wonderful.

Prior to boarding we didn't have any information about the sleeping arrangements; I had dreamed about a luxury cabin with circular windows overlooking the waves, maybe even an outside seating area just for us? But for the cheap price of the tickets, and mere upgrade cost, I reasoned that may have been a little too hopeful. I was indeed correct.

The staff gathered all of the guests into one large room consisting of cinema style seats and then rushed away. I assume, so that they could be far away before anyone vocalised their disappointment. The never-ending room was full of rows and rows of seats all facing forward, with minimal moving space between them. Cosy. Not wanting to reside in the evident luxury of "First Class," we quickly loaded our bags onto the metal shelving unit at the back of the room and set about exploring the ship. There were a few restaurants, a bar area, some souvenir shops, and a lot of locked doors.

After wandering aimlessly, and not particularly paying attention to the Tannoy system, we were not warmly greeted as we drifted into an Italian restaurant as it was about to close. They reluctantly agreed to serve us, which we were extremely thankful for, but only if we ordered instantly and ate fast. We apologetically agreed and didn't dare to ask any further questions.

Pasta and pizza scoffed, and wine sloshed on top, we thanked our irritated hosts and made our way to the bar, deciding that the only way we would get any sleep in that crowded cinema room would be if we were drunk (like we needed a reason to buy a drink). This meant choosing to ignore the sky-high prices and ordering a couple of glasses of copper-coloured wine. After a few more card games and a few too many overpriced acidic drinks, we stumbled back to the sleeping room, only this time to be hit with a chilling breeze. Instantly we were shivering. Full of hope, we peered through the darkness to our bags, which were now being blocked by a horizontal giant. We stared longingly at our Bag Of Wonders, willing it to come to us. Now would have been the perfect time to discover Matilda-style moving powers. Alas, it did not come zooming through the air and no matter how much we wished, the snoring gargantuan was not going to move without our interception, instead, he would remain as the barrier between us and anything warmer than shorts and t-shirts.

Without another option, we tiptoed over, and Ev tentatively reached across his rising abdomen. He managed to pull one of our clammy travel towels from a slightly open zip. That would have to do, even asleep this man showed an aggressive expression. We reasoned that sleep is when people are at their most peaceful, yet if they are prematurely woken, they become instantly angry, so if his starting stance was anger, who knows how he would have reacted to disturbance.

Most of the room was also already asleep, so we moved as quietly as we could to a pair of empty seats, slumping down for what we knew would be a long, frosty night. The room only got colder and the seats more uncomfortable, so in the end I resorted to sleeping on the hard floor beneath us whilst Ev took a stroll onto the outside deck. I caught a few hours of broken sleep, punctuated with zombie-like screen-scrolling. I braved the balance check, only to be hit with a hollowing realisation. We only had two hundred euros left.

Somehow since Germany we had managed to spend one thousand and three hundred euros on the credit card. I scanned the recent transactions fastidiously, hoping to find a charge that wasn't ours and consequently claw some money back, but of course it was all us. This new panic definitely didn't help with my desperate sleep battle.

I looked around to break the news to Ev, but he hadn't returned. He was dozing undisturbed overlooking the storm we had left behind. The following day, he explained the peacefulness of the empty deck compared with the electrical storm raging in the distance as being almost magical. I was gutted to have missed out, especially as my body ached from the contorted angles I had suffered through. Plus, I now had this huge money-worry looming over me.

When the morning finally dragged itself in, and as soon as sleeping beauty moved, I scurried over like a freezing feral rat and frantically layered up. Hair dishevelled and now far too many clothes on, I looked like I belonged to the streets, yet Ev still looked fresh and handsome. As he led me off the boat, I felt like his charity case, a gorgeous, bronzed man and his scruffy dependant.

We paced up and down cobbled roads, the backpack's rickety wheels clacking along behind us. Quickly we found a café, where my appearance invited many judging side-eyes, as we ate pastries galore. I shared the newest financial concern. Ev shrugged, "that's loads we've only got two more days."

I decided to leave the conversation there. So far, we'd spent our allotted nine hundred euros, plus a further one thousand three hundred on the credit card. So that totalled two thousand and two hundred, split across twenty days making our average daily spend one hundred and ten euros. So, it wasn't "loads" (weirdly it was just about what we *needed*) I definitely wouldn't be returning with any emergency credit left. One hundred per day isn't so bad, if you're on a weekend break, but when we consider that all of our accommodation and transport had already been paid for, that money had gone on unnecessarily fancy meals, and beer. We hadn't taken much to the backpacker life of cheap food and frugality and soon we'd have to pay for it. But for now, we had just two days left so we may as well enjoy them.

So unbelievably tired from all the travelling, and the most recent disrupted sleep, we were ready for our final stay of the trip, in an actual hotel. Not a tent, or a shared room, or a tin can, or a partly demolished apartment. A clean beach side hotel, with a sea view balcony.

Full of excitement, we bounded to the check-in desk, only to be told that our room was not ready and wouldn't be for quite some hours. Deflated, exhausted, and still looking like I was wearing everything I owned, we abandoned the bags and wandered down to the beach.

An immensely wide, flat, and golden empty beach sat before us. It was still so quiet as the day had barely begun. We laid down and tried to find comfort on the sand as we watched the sun proceed in its uphill climb above us. As time went on, the cold in my bones melted away, and the beach filled with marine divers and sandcastle architects. Ev, dressed appropriately, whipped off his top and dived into the shallows. I, however, who had never thought I would ever be warm again, had left behind my swimwear and shorts and instead bought jumper upon jumper so sat in a grubby slump. Stubborn with tiredness, I refused the two-minute walk back to the bag at the hotel and opted for a sulky sweat instead.

After a few more hot hours, our room was ready. A clean hotel room, with a sea view balcony, where now we could sit and drink wine and eat the olives. The perfect place to end our adventure.

Enigmatic Escapade

Quite unbelievably, the two days between arriving in Senigallia and the day we were due to leave were comparatively uneventful. We swam a lot, explored some ruins of sorts, dined out, and reminisced about all the chaos that had led us there. On the final night, we found a fancy restaurant and hoisted the credit card right to its limit. The previously untouched credit card we had agreed only to use in emergencies was now maxed out and we would have to pay it off once back home, but that was a problem for future us and by that point, it was too late so we may as well have spent it all.

However, the next morning, the more normal pattern of the trip returned. We arose early to check out, with plans to catch the first train running which would ensure we arrived at the airport promptly for our flight home. Simple? Yet we failed at the first hurdle.

Bags packed for the final time, we bounded to reception ready to check out and begin our journey home. I smiled as I handed back the room key and went to leave (forgetting that they had our passports locked safely away) when the shrill voice of the hotel receptionist instructed us to wait.

"You need to pay." She announced.

What? Why had I not already paid for the room? I had done so everywhere else. I stared at her quizzically. Her expression didn't falter.

"I have already, when I booked," I bravely broached the situation. "I think." I added that to sound less confrontational, but there was no think about it, I was sure.

"You have paid deposit; you still have one hundred and fifty-three euros to pay."

Ev and I looked at each other, eyes full of the uncomfortable knowledge that we had spent every last penny the previous night. We had nothing, no cash and no balance left on any card. The only real money we had was the sandy change in the bottom of our bags and there most definitely wasn't one hundred and fifty-three euros.

She then added that she cannot accept payments this early in the morning and we would have to wait half an hour for the computer payment something or other to be activated. Regardless of our inability to pay, it was such a flawed system, what if people (like us) had flights to catch. Or didn't want to sit for half an hour in a total panic about how they were going to pay. She was keeping us against our will, but we were too scared to argue. Even if she hurried the payment system it wouldn't change the fact that we had no money, so we sat, and panicked, and waited.

Quietly we discussed that our only option would be to try the maxed-out credit card and hope for the best. My brain flitted from panicking about the card being declined to panicking about missing the flight like an intense game of taunting ping-pong.

"The card won't work."

"You'll miss your flight."

"They'll be angry."

"You'll be stranded."

Back and forth the worries fought for my attention whilst I did my best to override them. *You can't control the future. Don't worry about things that are out of your hands.* These positive affirmations would have yielded more power if this situation wasn't wholly caused by my poor decision making and lack of attention to detail. There was far too much going on inside my mind for this early in the morning. I wondered if the same was happening within Ev's head. I looked at him to see if I could see any familiarity of how I was feeling. He had an uncomfortable expression, but it wasn't worry related, I knew that look; all that was on his mind was food.

If our passports weren't secure behind the desk, and the clearly-not-doing-anything-apart-from-making-us-wait staff weren't casually sauntering back and forth, we would have run. In hushed voices, we debated jumping over and snatching the passports back, but neither of us had the balls, or the skill to do so unwitnessed.

Definitely more than half an hour later, they beckoned us over to pay. Tentatively, I produced the maxed-out card and hoped for the best. Waiting for the payment to process was unbelievably painful, watching the loading circle swirl around and around was teasing my fretful mind. If it declined, we had no way to pay, so then what? Would we have to live here now? Owned by the hotel and locked in the dungeons?

That overly familiar high-pitched "ding!" erupted from their card machine. Somehow it worked!

How positively underwhelming. I had spent the last three weeks worrying about running out of money, and what would happen if we did. And now that had actually happened, nothing happened. I suppose that's true of all worries, all of mine anyway. They're fabricated "what ifs" that drain energy when in fact they never amount to anything. I'd wasted time and energy worrying about so many things on this trip, what if we miss the bus/coach/flight, what if the people are mean, what if we run out of money, or most irrational what if we die.

And now we had run out of money, and nothing happened. Not immediately anyway. I assumed, correctly, that a large fine would follow on the credit card bill, but for now, that didn't matter. We were free! One worry down, we could now continue our journey.

Anxiously, we raced to the train station and, of course, the train had already gone. We scanned the board for the next train and found one heading to the same end-destination our original train was, so we assumed this would be a safe bet. Not wanting to rely on the maxed-out card our only option was to use our intended tickets and feign ignorance if questioned.

Our flight time was racing closer, Time had finally woken up and was desperate to beat us to the airport. Already so delayed we were utterly relieved when the train pulled in. At last, we were on the way to the airport to fly home. We had enjoyed our trip so much, but all the disasters and panic were coming to an end, and it felt like we could finally relax and just reflect peacefully.

Unfortunately, that wasn't yet the case. Yes, the train was heading to the same destination, *but* it was not stopping at all of the stops. Or rather it did stop, but for no reason as the doors would not open and people weren't entering or exiting. It was some teasing version of a fast train. So, we saw the airport, stopped outside it briefly, frantically pressed the open-door button, and then continued to travel into the unknown cities of eastern Italy.

I could have cried as we watched more and more stops come and go whilst we were trapped inside this fast-moving prison. We were so lost, and so late. We'd lucked out once with the credit card, but we had no idea if that was just a one-off success or not. It was a very likely possibility that if/when this train ever ended, we'd have no money to get us back to the airport. On top of this, both of our phones were dead, because of course they were. Why wouldn't they be dead as we tore further and further into the unknown with absolutely everything apart from anything we needed.

More stops came and went as we sat impatiently, desperate to deboard.

My panic prevented me from talking, and his facial expressions made it clear that Ev was finally feeling the same, or the hunger had totally taken over. I could see no light at the end of this never-ending train ride.

When at last the train stopped for real, we bundled our things together and stepped out to Who-Knows-Where. We thankfully avoided being questioned about our tickets, so apprehensively followed the crowd and made our way through the station and out onto the street.

This trip had its problems, voluminous problems, yet with little intervention from us, it had an unfathomable way of solving them too, and in true, consistent fashion, here is the last way:

As we exited the station, there was a queue of people boarding a bus. A shuttle bus directly to the airport. Not Milan airport or Pisa or Bologna airport. But Ancona airport, our desired destination. A bus that was due to leave as soon as all the passengers were on board. We joined the end of the queue and waited until our turn to be served. Nervously, we asked how much the tickets were. The driver looked us up and down, and upon seeing the desperation in our eyes, gave a very low price of five euros each.

This was a cash only transaction. His worn-out leather wallet and lack of technology confirmed that. I was certain we didn't have that much, no way could that have gone unspent. Much to the ticker master's surprise, we tipped the entire contents of our backpacks out onto the cobbled pavement and anxiously accumulated all of our loose coins, which totalled.... exactly ten euros!

Unbelievable.

I felt suspicious of our good luck and once again wondered if someone was watching, waiting to prank us.

Completely elated, we passed over all the filthy coins and pranced gleefully on board. We were still very late, but at least this mode of transport was actually taking us to where we needed to be. We had no idea how long the journey would take so settled down and gazed out of the window. I nestled my head into Ev's shoulder and tried to enjoy the passing scenery whilst my brain forcefully inflicted more unnecessary fear.

"We did it!" I whispered, never before had I felt such a sense of achievement at the end of a holiday.

"Not quite, we've still got to get home." Ev joked.

I ignored the joke and set about whittling away the journey in my usual way, "Would you rather-"

"I wouldn't." He interrupted.

"What?"

"I wouldn't rather and I'd do nothing." He finally put an end to my incessant question asking.

Stunned silent I let my mind drift in and out of weary dreams.

Surprisingly, we did finally make it to the airport, *and* we hadn't missed the flight. Once on board we tried the card again, and yet again it went through, (and yet again I was fined,) but at least we were able to eat as we reminisced about our whirlwind adventure.

Although it was only twenty-two days, it felt like we had been away for a lifetime. We'd been lost, hungry and in fear of our lives, but also had laughed and danced and smiled more than ever. We'd met many weird, mean and lecherous people, and made some great friends. And best of all, we'd not been out of each other's company for more than an hour at a time, romantic not so much, but it was definitely some of the solid groundwork for our chaotic relationship.

We re-lived the madness endlessly as we heard the comfort of home calling our names. No more fear of missing buses or running out of money (as it was all gone), but also no more adventure for a while.

Ev had been completely lifted out of his post-op slump. Whether he liked it or not he'd had to navigate, console and rework his way through my *faultless* itinerary. The new purpose and sudden responsibility of our wellbeing had brought him completely back to himself, which was more than I could have hoped for.

I came home lighter, (the lack of our blow-up mattress contributed to this significantly,) I had (accidently) found myself in many situations that were out of my comfort zone and way out of my control. Things had gone wrong, but nothing bad happened when they did. I didn't drop down dead or burst into flames. I had panicked but I'd also pushed through, and just like that I was back home to share the chaos. I was lighter of worry and hoped to stay that way.

A fitting end to an enigmatic escapade.

Oh, how I wish we'd learnt the downfalls of over-planning and under-saving on this trip before we set off to Southeast Asia.....

THERE'S ALWAYS A DRAMA

LUCY WHITE

NO ENTRY

The second book in this series follows us through Vietnam, Cambodia, and Thailand. Another over-planned trip that was destined to fall apart. More dramas occur but this time we're much further from the comforts of home and without the emergency credit card to bail us out.

Poor timing leaves us moving with the rainy season, initially limiting our island-hopping dreams. Instead, we're submerged into moped filled cities, desperately avoiding work placements. Soon enough we make our way to the beach but not before a huge visa dilemma, and a very real fear of being homeless.

From senseless downpours to huge venomous snakes, to stony faced border officials to well-disguised party drugs we were determined not to let anything ruin our fun. Little did we know that the fun stopped at just the right time.

COMING SOON

REFLECTIONS OF A CALAMAITY (SERIES)

THERE'S ALWAYS A DRAMA

NO ENTRY (coming soon)

About the Author

Hi, I'm Lucy White an anxiety fuelled writer.

Travelling is my passion, albeit one I'm not very good at, and writing is the outlet that keeps me sane.

Through writing this travelogue I was able to relive our treasured adventure and came to the realisation that I was destined to return home traumatised by my own dramatic narratives when in fact I should have been having fun.

My over-anxious inner monologues had the capability to create further problems and lay upon a recurring fear of death during our time of freedom- now totally laughable, as I wonder at the curiosity that is the mind.

This is the first book in my Reflections Of A Calamity series. The second, "No Entry", will be released in 2024. It documents our three-month stint through Southeast Asia and the *many* dramas that we faced.

In the meantime, keep up to date with our chaos by visiting my website, www.lucywhite.xyz for travel photos and short stories, many that were touched upon throughout this book.

Printed in Great Britain
by Amazon